The Urgent Need for *The Certainty Cure*

"Having had the privilege of working with Stefani, I know firsthand the depth of wisdom, care, and integrity she brings to her work. In a culture drowning in reactions — outrage, finger-pointing, and endless diagnosis — Stefani stands out as a rare and necessary voice of solutions. *The Certainty Cure* is not just another commentary on polarization; it is a blueprint for healing it. Stefani doesn't stop at exposing our addiction to being right — she offers a practical and hopeful path to move beyond it. With honesty and courage, she shows us how intellectual vulnerability can rebuild trust, strengthen relationships, and transform division into connection. This book is a timely and valuable guide for anyone seeking a healthier, more constructive way forward."

— *Rich Diviney, Bestselling Author and Retired Navy SEAL CDR*

"In *The Certainty Cure*, Stefani Ruper shows how our obsession with being right divides families, communities, and the nation, and how curiosity and vulnerability can bring us back together. Thoughtful, hopeful, and deeply practical, it offers a way forward for anyone who wants to heal what has been broken between us."

— *Simon Greer, Founder, Bridging the Gap & Host of Courageous Conversations at TNP*

THE CERTAINTY CURE

Heal Polarization and Grow in an Age of Addiction to Being Right

by

Stefani Ruper

On the Way Books, 2025

Copyright © 2025 Stefani Ruper
All rights reserved. No part of this publication may be reproduced without prior permission of the author, except in the case of brief quotations in reviews or scholarly works.

Published by *On the Way Books*

ISBN: 979-8-9935375-0-4

Library of Congress Control Number: 2025927025

For my father, Greg Ruper,
who taught me to love what is,
and to live for what could be.

Table of Contents

Preface

Loving Thy Neighbor 9

Introduction

How Certainty Hurt Me and Could Be Hurting You 13

Chapter one

**Kissing Goodbye to a Toxic Dependency:
The Need to Be Right** 29

Chapter two

5 Signs You're in a Certainty Trap, and How to Get Out 43

Chapter three

The Life- and World-Changing Power of "I Don't Know" 57

Chapter four

10 Ways to Choose Growth Over Being Right 67

Chapter five

How to Talk Across Any Divide: A Practical Guide 81

Chapter six

**The Gift of Re-Imagining Truth as Imperfect
& On The Way** 97

Chapter seven

**Improve Your Intellect by Healing Your Heart
(Cultivating Inner Safety)** 111

Chapter eight

If You Want to Persuade, Stop Trying to Persuade 127

Chapter nine

Strengthening Scholarship & Society with Uncertainty 141

Chapter ten

**Beyond Politics: How Intellectual Vulnerability Transforms
Health, Inner Peace, and Spirit** 155

Conclusion

Why Not Try? 174

Appendices

Some Further Reading 179

Acknowledgments 181

PREFACE
Loving Thy Neighbor

I finished this book and was about to send it to the printers on September 12, 2025. The day Charlie Kirk—a political activist and the founder of Turning Point USA—was shot. I was on the beach having a picnic with my boyfriend. He got a text and gave me the news.

I have a confession to make: I have long hesitated to share the thoughts in this book because I knew I would lose friends and colleagues.

But it seems to me the buck must stop somewhere. And for me, it is here.

On the surface, this book is about political dialogue. It is a guidebook on how to talk to each other. It is about cultivating the skills to speak to one another freely, kindly, and productively.

Yet on a deeper level, it is a book about love.

More than anything, it is a call to, and set of instructions for, loving one another as neighbors.

I believe this is the only sustainable solution to our problem of polarization.

So far, I have encountered very few tools for this. Everybody agrees that polarization is a problem. A few bold souls advocate for constructive exchange, empathy, and mutual respect. But they are a mere few, and meanwhile, the solution most seem to strive for is *defeat the other side.*

Defeat, however, is a quest for dominance and control. It says *my side is surely right; yours has no value. You must change so you think, feel, and hope the way I do.* This is a kind of erasure.

I understand why people feel this way and put themselves at war with one another. As you'll read about later, I once did it. Many of my closest friends still do. But it is a threat to our safety and to our capacity to keep the fragile, imperfect, and tentative experiment of democracy alive.

It seems to me that the problems we face—animosity, distrust, stalled dialogue, talking past one another, and, now as of yesterday, assassination—will not be solved by fighting.

Fighting, in my experience, does not usually lead to less fighting. Fighting usually leads to more fighting.

What about loving?

Will loving help?

I wonder about this.

I once read that love is patient. It is kind. It does not envy. It does not boast. It is not proud. It does not dishonor others. It is not self-seeking. It is not easily angered. It keeps no record of wrongs.

And because of these qualities, love never fails.

It seems to me that loving one another according to this ethos includes decentering yourself, by which I mean: releasing your own needs and desires for a moment to get curious about this other person in front of you. To see and honor them in their own being, as you wish to be seen and honored in yours. To remember that they are just as human, just as squishy, just as vulnerable to pain, just as hopeful about the future, just as desperate to feel at home in the world, as you.

It seems to me that we could use a little bit more of this.

In the following pages, I invite you to set yourself aside a little bit. Not to abandon your values, beliefs, or convictions, but to release your absolute certitude about them.

In doing so, I suggest that this will not be the end of the world for you, or for us as a society, but a fresh beginning.

When we release certainty, we open ourselves to greater understanding. We multiply opportunities for growth. We equip ourselves to connect more fully. We experience more trust and homecoming in the world. We find new solutions to old problems.

It can take a little bit of courage to make this switch—from certainty to curiosity.

But it is, I believe, where real, radical love begins, and the fertile ground for all the good stuff that comes after.

INTRODUCTION

How Certainty Hurt Me and Could Be Hurting You

"You are so damn irrational!" I screamed at my dad.

I clenched my teeth. I didn't want to be erupting at him. But I couldn't stop the rush of furious words from bursting through the meager dam of my self-control.

I was just so mad.

To understand how I got to that moment of screaming, I need to take you back to a few years before it.

In 2006, I had left the small, Republican corner of southeast Michigan where I'd grown up listening to Rush Limbaugh call feminists "feminazis" to attend a liberal arts college on the east coast.

Four months later, I returned home for the Christmas holidays a vegetarian, subscribed to the *New York Times*, and trying to get Dad to watch Al Gore's climate change documentary *An Inconvenient Truth* with me.

Needless to say, Dad was not interested. I felt offended and indignant. Didn't he want to know what I'd learned? Didn't he know—or want to have his eyes opened to—how important this was? I felt certain that I was right, and he was wrong. I desperately wanted him to see what I saw. When he didn't, I felt rage, disappointment, and a roiling, indignant compulsion to convince him I was right.

Today, I see a lot more of what was going on that Christmas break than I did at the time. Throughout childhood and adolescence, I had hero-worshipped my father and taken everything he'd said as gospel. By the time I'd set off for college, we had a tight bond over shared values: hard work, self-determination, and personal liberty. Because of this, we understood one another as comrades: fellow warriors in a battle for a better, freer world.

After I went off to Dartmouth (which Dad was jokingly okay with because it was the most conservative Ivy League School), I started changing. Not only did I begin to explore new viewpoints, but I also began to think of myself as a different kind of person with different beliefs, values, and allegiances.

I began to change who I was.

When I went home for Christmas, I tried to make my dad change along with me.

I failed.

And I continued to fail in the exact same way for the next several years. This strained our whole family. Every gathering guaranteed at least one blowup. My brothers began to sit down for family dinners holding their breath, eyes darting between Dad and me. *When is Stefani going to lose it at Dad?*

But then in my late twenties it hit me: the problem wasn't Dad. It was me.

The more I had pushed, the more he'd resisted. Of course he had. Do you like it when friends and family members talk to you like you're ignorant—or evil? I know I don't.

So I began to try something different: just sitting with him. Not trying to convince him of anything. Just listening. Being respectful. I asked questions and shared from my perspective when it seemed appropriate. But that was it. No pressure on him to be won over; no attachment to outcomes on my part.

And something remarkable happened. Not only did our conversations become calmer, but they became richer. I started to see his perspective as a unique window onto the world—one that could challenge and expand my own thinking. Growing up, I had been wrong to take everything he'd said as gospel. But I began to realize it had also been wrong to start taking everything my peers or professors said as gospel, too.

When I started genuinely listening to my dad, I began learning from him again. He opened my eyes to new perspectives that my friends and colleagues who already agreed with me literally couldn't.

My understanding became so much richer.

After going through this with him, I began to open up like this with everybody. I stopped approaching conversations thinking, *What can I prove?* And instead: *What can I learn?*

I did this with people at the supermarket, out at bars, walking the streets of my neighborhood. I began to wonder:

What do they believe? Why? What have they seen and been through that has given them this set of beliefs, the same way what I've seen and been through has given me mine?

No matter a person's education, cultural location, apparent erudition, anything—I started approaching them as treasure troves of insight.

I hadn't anticipated it, but making this change was about to rewire my whole being.

Because in that process, I hadn't only discovered that I could improve my relationships with people. I realized that I'd been living with a constellation of intellectual habits that had been limiting my entire life. I'd gone through my first few decades with a compulsive need to be right, feeling like disagreement was a threat to my very identity, and stuck in a cycle of chasing safety through intellectual justification.

I was unearthing something much more fundamental—and damaging—in my relationship with beliefs.

The Addiction That's Isolating, Embattling, and Hurting Us

I now understand: I had been trapped in certainty addiction.

I was, as many people are, chasing emotional safety in righteousness. I subconsciously thought:

I am surely right. Therefore, I know who I am and who my allies are. I am justified. I know my place in the world and what's going to save us all.

It gave me peace.

Or, at least, a facsimile of peace.

The problem with certainty is that it does not, in fact, exist. We can't be fully certain of anything. So the more I chased it, the more I alienated myself from the things that would actually make me safer: fellowship, connection, mutual respect, curiosity, growth, and trust.

As I alienated myself from these things, I felt less safe, so I chased certainty even harder. And this narrowed my world further. I now understand that when you pin your identity, belonging, and security on a certain vision for the world being right, anything that seems like it might even marginally contradict that vision becomes a threat. The scope of things that feel safe to you narrows, and the scope of things that feel threatening to you grows.

So I felt peace when I read materials by or spent time with people who shared my beliefs. But the number of ideas and people I felt comfortable with got smaller and smaller. The degree of agreement required to be "in" got bigger and bigger.

No matter how kind, honorable, or well-intentioned someone on the "other side" was, if they didn't share my increasingly narrow vision for the world, they were the enemy.

So screw 'em.

The Costs of Certainty Addiction

What's being sacrificed in this war for righteousness? Families are becoming estranged from one another. A national survey recently revealed that 21% of Americans have become estranged from a family member, with 22% blocking a family member on social media and 19% skipping a family event due to disagreements on controversial topics.

This impact grows generation by generation. Approximately 48% of people 18–34 have reported arguing with a family member about a controversial issue, highlighting a heightened sensitivity to political differences in this demographic.

The number of politically mixed marriages in America has declined significantly, from about 30% in 2016 to 21% in 2020, reflecting the growing importance of political alignment in personal relationships.

And this is wearing us down. A significant majority of Americans express negative emotions when thinking about politics, with 65% reporting feeling "always or often exhausted" by politics and 55% feeling "always or often angry." This emotional strain often spills over into personal relationships, further deepening divides.

Beyond social health, certainty addiction also impacts our personal health and quality of life. Certainty obstructs productive curiosity about health, diet, self-image, lifestyle, purpose, career, the meaning of life, spiritual beliefs, etc.

What might you be overlooking or unaware of that's in the way of your flourishing?

What new possibilities could open up—for your relationships, and for your personal peace and growth—by trading certainty for curiosity?

Certainty addiction turns us into iron rods: rigid, unbending, seemingly strong. But iron corrodes. And so, over time, do we.

What if there's another, better way to be strong?

The Antidote: Intellectual Vulnerability

There's a way to break free from certainty addiction and begin cultivating that strength: an intellectual practice I call intellectual vulnerability.

Intellectual vulnerability is:
- accepting that you, like the rest of us, don't have all the answers;
- welcoming that learning only happens when we talk with people different from us;
- celebrating that we devise optimal solutions when we work with, not against, people different from us.

It's Not Mere Intellectual Humility

Intellectual vulnerability is not intellectual humility, which says "I might be wrong." It's intellectual *vulnerability*, which says:

"I know I'm wrong, or at least that I don't have all the answers. Please help open my eyes to what I'm missing."

Intellectual humility is passive. Intellectual vulnerability is proactive. It fully accepts, and even welcomes, that each of our own personal perspectives is limited, and therefore seeks to improve it through exposure to others:

"I need insight from your perspective to help me grow my own."

Think about how this plays out in real conversation.

Intellectual humility might sound like: "Well, I suppose I could be wrong about climate policy, but let me tell you why I still think my approach is best..." It acknowledges fallibility but remains defensive.

Intellectual vulnerability sounds different: "I'm sure there are things about climate policy I'm not seeing clearly. Here's what I'm seeing. What do you see? What might I be missing? What experiences have shaped your perspective that I haven't had?"

One hedges; the other opens. One protects your position while paying lip service to doubt; the other genuinely invites correction and expansion. The difference is the difference between cracking a door and flinging it wide open.

Intellectual Vulnerability Math

I took my first step towards intellectual vulnerability when one day it suddenly hit me: there are eight billion people on this planet, and every single one of them, myself included, thinks they're right about everything.

I realized that even though I felt like I had all the answers, I felt that way because I'd only ever observed the world from my own perspective. I'd only ever witnessed events from within the little bubble of my own experience. I'd made the best sense I could from that vantage point: I'd drawn the conclusions I'd drawn as a kid because of what I'd been exposed to, and then as a student in college because of what I'd been exposed to, and then as an adult because of what I'd been exposed to. Today, my professional philosophical opinion is that I had (at least some) free will through this process of sense-making, but I also know I have never, not once, been able to think beyond the confines of what I've personally witnessed, been through, or read, etc.

Not once.

Other people are exactly the same. They've drawn the conclusions they've drawn because of what they've witnessed and experienced, from behind their own eyes. Their beliefs about God and the meaning of life, political obligations and liberties, the trustworthiness of various authorities or institutions, what's humane and will bring about the most peace, freedom, health, and happiness: it all comes from what they've seen and experienced. Simple as that.

We learn best when we widen, not narrow, what we see

Imagine being born into a cult. Would you gain more understanding of reality by staying put and entrenching yourself in what you presently believe, or by breaking free and exploring other perspectives?

We are all like this: cult-esque. If you were born in a relatively more democratic and open society, you've experienced less authoritarian control than people born in cults, but we all share the fundamental limit of being just one set of eyes making sense of the world from one very tiny slice of the human experience pie.

I began to realize: the difficult but liberating truth is that the odds that I am the one person who's got everything figured out better than everyone else are one in eight billion: 1/8,000,000,000, or 0.0000000125%.

So if I wanted to discover the honest truth of things, I wouldn't find it by burrowing further into my own views. Neither would I find it by talking exclusively with people who had similar outlooks to me. I'd find it by busting out and engaging people with different outlooks.

Nowadays, I think of beliefs like maps of reality. The process of forming beliefs is essentially a process of sketching a map of reality. But maps aren't the territory they try to capture. They are approximations. They aren't guaranteed to be accurate. In fact, they will *always* lack at least some amount of detail about the territory they try to depict.

Through life, each of us has drawn (and is continuing to draw) our own maps from our personal vantage points. Understanding this, I now do my best to refrain from asking myself: *how can I prove the superiority of my own map?* And instead ask: *what are others seeing that I literally can't?*

I began to wonder, and now invite you to wonder with me: Are we better served by clinging to our own beliefs and fighting with one another about who's right, shouting about the superiority of the view from our own mountaintops, or by loosening our grip, respecting each other as equally honorable seekers of truth, and finding out what the world looks like according to people on mountaintops over *there*?

I Don't Know, Help Me Grow.

It's an oversimplification, but one excellent mantra for intellectual vulnerability is *I don't know, Help me grow.*

Saying this isn't a sign of weakness. It's a source of magnificent strength. One long-held cultural truism is "Knowledge is power." And it surely is. Knowledge is insight into reality. When we have insight into reality, we can use it to get the outcomes we want. That's power.

But where does knowledge come from?

Ignorance.

There is no such thing as knowledge without the ignorance from which it springs.

We never gain knowledge without first accepting we don't have it, or at least that we don't see the complete picture.

"I know" doesn't exist without first admitting "I don't fully know."

What's more, the more easily and readily we say "I don't fully know"—that is, to admit we have blind spots—the more quickly we fill them in. We grow more. We understand more. We gain insight into the myriad possible ways of understanding reality, experiencing reality, and living and working with people in that reality.

The quest for knowledge is one that never ends. Most mistakenly assume that once you learn a fact or a perspective, that's the end of it, but the truth is possibilities for learning and growth—regarding any topic—are never-ending.

Benefits of Intellectual Vulnerability

As we release certainty and begin to say more "I don't know, help me grow," we create space for genuine change:

Social & Political

More nuanced conversations. Without the pressure to defend fixed positions, discussions can explore complexity rather than advocate for sides. You can more fully hear what others are saying instead of preparing your rebuttal.

Resilience against manipulation. Those who profit off your anger and fear lose their power when you're not desperately seeking certainty from their content. You become harder to exploit.

Space for genuine connection. When both people in a conversation can admit they don't have all the answers, real dialogue becomes possible. Relationships can be about mutual discovery rather than mutual convincing.

Reduced social anxiety. When you cease performing intellectual perfection, a significant source of social stress disappears. You can show up as yourself rather than your positions.

Personal & Emotional

Freedom from exhaustion. The constant vigilance required to defend your worldview against all challenges is draining. Intellectual vulnerability offers relief from that hypervigilance.

Reduced shame about changing your mind. Change stops feeling like failure and starts feeling like strength.

Improved outcomes and solutions across domains of life. When you're not locked into proving your approach is the only right one in your work, relationships, physical health, spiritual health, and community involvement, you more readily unlock new solutions.

These aren't guaranteed outcomes. But they're possibilities that open up when we stop needing to be right.

But, but, but....

One of the most common, and understandable, sources of resistance to intellectual vulnerability is:

But THEIR approach is inhumane. My approach is the truly humane one. This isn't "just politics." Suffering, injustice, and the fate of humanity are at stake.

It's true: there's no such thing as "just politics." Most people are very emotionally attached to their views of things, and for good reason. They believe their views will lead to the most safe and just future. I count myself one of them.

It's also true that sometimes people are subject to an egregious amount of manipulation, or have undergone an egregious amount of suffering—and have in the course of these things become relatively less capable of considering the feelings of others, and relatively more capable of intending harm towards others.

But a number of phenomena I'll cautiously call *facts* render intellectual vulnerability the best way to handle our differences:

1) These cases of extreme intolerance, animus, and inhumanity are far less common than it seems at first glance. Most people are just as well-intentioned and have just as strong hopes for the future as you do.
2) Most people love truth just as much as you do, even if they don't see it your way or as "clearly."
3) Your deep love for your values and vision for the future drives you to suspicion of people who don't share it; this is the same force in others driving their suspicion of you.
4) Most of us share the same values: truth, safety, love, justice, education, health, etc, but because of what we've experienced and how we've learned to make sense of the world, have different ways of trying to honor those values.
5) Approaching one another with animosity will never solve our conflict or reduce ignorance. It will only create more conflict and deepen ignorance.
6) If you want people to understand your values, the best path is to share them with kindness and empathy for *their* values.

It's crucial to boundary against violence, dominance, and attitudes that prohibit mutually enriching conversations.

Beyond that, as much as any of us love our views and values, the path ahead is learning *more* about one another and where we come from. Not less.

This is, at least, my little thought, and little hope.

How to Use This Guide

When I first started practicing intellectual vulnerability with my dad, I would have loved a roadmap. This handbook is meant to work like that. I offer ideas I hope spark your curiosity about the nature of beliefs and truth, but more than anything I want to give you practical tools.

So this book is primarily a guide for practice, reflection, and experimentation. Think of it as a gym for your mind: the exercises are the workouts, the reflection prompts are the stretches, and the examples are the models to learn from.

Here's how to get the most out of it:

Reflect. Don't rush. Take time with each chapter and with yourself. This stuff takes time. Let it simmer. If you don't like something I say, stay curious about why and potentially revisit it later to see if it strikes the same chord. Notice which sections spark curiosity, resistance, or surprise. Your emotional reactions may be clues to where intellectual vulnerability is most needed.

Try the exercises. Every chapter includes exercises or prompts. These aren't optional extras if you really want to cultivate intellectual vulnerability (to be clear, no pressure)—

they're the core of the practice. Approach them with curiosity, not performance. You're not proving yourself "right" or "wrong"; you're exploring your own thinking.

Practice the mini-habits. Change happens incrementally. Pick one small practice at a time—questioning yourself before others, leaning into discomfort, listening with full attention—and build it into your daily life.

Experiment with others. Conversations are where growth really happens. Try offering a perspective, asking curious questions, or simply listening without judgment. Notice how it feels to shift from debate to mutual learning and enrichment.

Don't self-shame or call your questions silly. There's no such thing as a "silly question." There's no shame in feeling awkward. If this stuff is new for you, you're bound to feel a bit unnatural at first. Great. Keep going. Don't shame yourself for trying. Celebrate it.

Above all, remember: this guide is about process, not perfection. The goal is not to have all the answers or to never be wrong. The goal is to be willing to learn, to expand your understanding, and to live in a way that makes space for curiosity, connection, and growth—your own, and that of everyone you engage with.

.

Tip: *Choose curiosity over certainty. Today, try asking one question about a belief you think you already "know." Listen more than you respond. Your mind grows in the gaps you don't yet understand.*

CHAPTER ONE

Kissing Goodbye to a Toxic Dependency: The Need to Be Right

In This Chapter, You Will...
-Begin to understand why certainty feels so intoxicating and is so dangerous
-See how the brain rewards certainty, why certainty functions like an addiction, and how media profit from keeping us outraged and divided
-Explore the deeper hunger beneath certainty: the longing for safety, belonging, meaning, and connection
-Learn small but practical steps for loosening your grip on being right and choosing curiosity instead, even when it feels risky

Why Being Wrong Feels Dangerous

The first step to overcoming certainty addiction is understanding it—and that means examining why our minds cling so desperately to being right. Why are we so afraid of being wrong or unsure? And why do we feel so threatened by people who disagree with us?

There's one reason many of us are familiar with: looking stupid. We don't want to look stupid. So we perform a kind of intellectual invincibility, both while speaking with others and also internally in our own minds.

But there's a deeper reason that's far more primal and powerful: being wrong shakes the ground beneath our feet.

When we discover we've been mistaken or feel unsure about something that matters—who we are, what kind of world we live in, or how others see us—our foundations tremble. Reality can begin to feel unstable.

This disruption usually feels uncomfortable. In studies where experimenters intentionally knock people off kilter—by swapping one study facilitator out for another wearing the same clothes, for example, or by having them read absurdist stories—most people report feeling uncomfortable yet struggle to articulate what's wrong. Even if they don't express it or consciously recognize their distress, they exhibit biological signs of heightened stress such as increased skin conductance.

Experimental psychologist Travis Proulx and colleagues call this experience *absurdity*. They were following precedent, as existentialist philosophers had already used the word to describe the link between uncertainty and deep existential discomfort. Kierkegaard defined absurdity as the condition of being forced to believe without certainty, and it was *dizzying*; Sartre described absurdity as the unknowability of things, and it was *nauseating*; Camus said nature was *silent* and *primitively hostile* in its inaccessibility to us; he named the philosophy he devised to help us cope with this *absurdism*.

When sensibility is shaken, *we* are shaken.

This is deeply uncomfortable, often intolerable.

I also know this because I've lived it.

Hero Worship, Politics, and the Near-Shattering of a Family

As mentioned, I grew up hero-worshipping my Republican father. We'd ride in the car together listening to Rush Limbaugh talk radio. I'd soak up every word feeling grounded, safe, and part of something bigger than myself. Then I went off to college and started to change, as well as to try to get my dad to change along with me. We started fighting the first Christmas break I came home from liberal arts college, in the winter of 2006.

One fight a few years after that stands out in my memory. It was about racial disparities in incarceration rates. I shoved a volume of the encyclopedia in his face.

"Look, you unrelentingly stubborn ass, it's statistics! You can't ignore statistics!"

"You can't trust everything you read! You don't know who wrote that!"

"It's. The. *ENCYCLOPEDIA!!!!*"

I have never yelled at anyone in my life the way I did at my father in that fight. After I shouted about the encyclopedia, I clenched my fists, inhaled and exhaled heavily with my nostrils flaring, and swallowed the stream of insults pressing against my teeth. I counted to five. Then I gritted out: "Fine! I'll go! Fine! See you later!"

I walked out and slammed the door, furious—but beneath the fury was desperation.

I didn't know how to love him and disagree at the same time.

A bit later, my older brother wearily expressed to me: "Our family is going to fall apart."

He didn't say it, but the implication was thick in the air: *And it's going to be your fault.*

Certainty as a Drug

In the introduction, I called certainty "addictive." That word is not accidental. I chose it with careful consideration. Certainty addiction is more subtle and has less biochemical punch than classical addictions, especially substance addictions, but like classical addictions, certainty addiction is driven by emotional pain and fear.

For me, I had become terrified that my dad's "side" was going to win the battle for our political future. I felt real, deep fear of what seemed to be his vision for the world. I was also hurt by the new distance between him and me. I felt alone and, in a sense, betrayed, because Dad refused to be persuaded by me.

This drove me into an increasingly strong compulsion to be right about things. This didn't just alienate me from my dad, but also from curiosity, from learning, and from growth.

That is part of the great irony and tragedy of certainty addiction, just like other addictions:

I used it to chase the feeling of safety, but in doing so I made myself less safe.

When we defend our beliefs—especially ones we feel passionately about—our brains reward us with a sense of safety and rightness. The relief feels good, like scratching an itch or winning an argument. For a moment, the world feels ordered, safe, and manageable. We've established our position, secured our identity, and pushed back against the discomfort of absurdity.

But like other quick fixes, the satisfaction fades quickly. The relief is temporary, and soon we need another hit of rightness to feel secure again. We seek out more confirmation, more validation, more proof that we're on the right side. We get stuck in the cycle.

One unique aspect of certainty addiction compared to more classical addictions is that certainty performs a specific psychological function that we naturally lean on, especially times of uncertainty and stress. It helps prop up three pillars of psychological stability: identity, belonging, and control.

Concerning identity, our beliefs tell us who we are and the role we play in the world. Certainty about such thing feels great. It helps hold us steady in a world that feels complex and unsteady.

Concerning belonging, beliefs often dictate the groups we belong to. We naturally form allegiances according to the visions we have for the world. This can knit us into very tight communities while signaling who is "with us" and who is not. Certainty often promises safety inside the circle—even (or especially) if it requires shutting others out.

Concerning control, the unknown can feel intolerable, even threatening. When we feel our vision for the world is certainly righteous, we feel as if we've secured the ground beneath our feet. Everything can and should unfold as we expect.

In any moment of hurt or fear, we can retreat to certainty to hold us steady in our identity, belonging, and sense of control. Doing this can become deeply habituated.

But like any drug, the relief is fleeting. The more we rely on it, the more dependent we become.

And certainty is a drug we can take anywhere, anytime, at the push of a thought.

The Political Dangers of Certainty

The feeling of safety we get from righteousness is an illusion.

The very behaviors that make us feel protected—sticking to our side, shaming dissenters, avoiding uncertainty—make us more vulnerable to manipulation, misunderstanding, and stagnation.

History offers vivid warnings:

European Wars of Religion (1524-1648): Catholics and Protestants were each certain they held the only path to salvation. This made compromise more difficult and dialogue heretical. Geopolitical conflict drove much of the warfare in this era, but religious certainty enabled and prolonged the devastation. The result was decades of warfare that devastated Europe, killing millions in conflicts that might have been avoided through intellectual humility.

Rejection of Handwashing in Hospitals (1840s-1880s): When Hungarian doctor Ignaz Semmelweis noticed that wards staffed by doctors had much higher death rates from childbed fever than those staffed by midwives, he proposed a radical solution: between patient visits, doctors should wash their hands with chlorine solution. But the medical establishment was certain that "gentlemen's hands" couldn't carry disease—after all, they were educated professionals, not common laborers. Their certainty about professional dignity and medical knowledge prevented them from considering evidence that contradicted their self-image, leading to countless preventable deaths that continued for decades.

Resistance to Continental Drift Theory: When German meteorologist Alfred Wegener proposed in 1912 that continents had once been joined and had drifted apart over millions of years, he presented compelling evidence: matching fossils across oceans, similar rock formations on different continents, and the puzzle-like fit of continental coastlines. But the geological community was certain they understood how the Earth worked: continents were fixed, permanent features anchored to the ocean floor. Leading geologists dismissed Wegener's theory not because they had better evidence, but because it violated their fundamental assumptions about planetary mechanics. They couldn't imagine a force powerful enough to move entire continents, so they refused to seriously consider the mounting evidence. It took nearly fifty years and the discovery of plate tectonics to vindicate Wegener's insights, during which time geological understanding stagnated because the scientific community was too certain of what was "impossible."

These examples show that certainty addiction isn't limited to any particular worldview—they can affect religious and secular thinking, ancient beliefs and modern science. When we become too attached to being right, we lose the ability to learn, adapt, and grow.

When Disagreement Becomes War

It is easier to fall into certainty addiction than ever before. Traditional and social media platforms have discovered that emotionally charged content keeps us engaged longer than calm, nuanced discussion. The more activated we feel—whether angry, afraid, or righteously indignant—the more likely we are to click, share, comment, and return for more.

This is the attention economy: media platforms compete for our attention, because having our attention means they can show us ads, and that yields profit. So we've been given, or have been enabled to perpetuate, oversimplified, villainized images of one another largely because it's profitable.

Our natural inclination to seek safety in certitude is easily manipulable, especially if we're unaware of what's happening. So as we feel increasingly unsafe in this media-driven frenzy, we entrench ourselves further in our own views. We see ideological opponent more one-dimensionally, and we erect more defenses.

For many today, every conversation feels like a battle in the war for the future of the world. People who disagree with you aren't just misguided, anymore—they're evil, your *enemies*.

And most think they've chosen to be in this war. But because our need for safety makes us vulnerable to manipulation by attention economy profiteers (and politicians and other powerful figures), the truth is that it's largely chosen us.

It's happened *to* us.

How real is our collective conviction that we're in the righteous group and under attack from a villainous or naive other?

Fortunately, with awareness, perspective, and tools like the ones I provide in this book, we have the ability to make ourselves more resilient to such influences. We can love one another, learn from each other, and thrive together regardless of our technological and political landscapes.

That change begins with understanding the hunger at the root of it all.

The Real Hunger Beneath Certainty

When we peel back certainty, we discover truth itself is not quite the real craving. Beneath the drive for certainty lies a hunger for the safety of trust, belonging, and meaning.

We cling to beliefs because they feel like scaffolding for our existence. When those beliefs are threatened, it's not just our opinions at stake—it's our sense of who we are and whether we matter. Certainty is a fortress we build against danger, chaos, loneliness, and fear.

But that fortress comes at a cost: rigidity, brittleness, isolation. The more we cling, the more fragile our trust becomes. We think we're building necessary defenses, but we're actually cutting ourselves off from connection and the growth that results—both for us and for others.

The craving for certainty is really a craving to be seen, understood, accepted, and secure—even when we falter. To feel that life has coherence and that we will be safe in a vast and mysterious world.

Understanding this hunger can help us reconfigure how we relate to beliefs. We don't have to cling to them. We can find our safety somewhere else—somewhere healthier, more sustainable, and more likely to lead to peace and progress.

That place is in openness, vulnerability, and the willingness to learn, love, and grow.

Recognizing that the craving for certainty is a craving for relational and existential nourishment empowers us to respond differently. Instead of seeing disagreement as a threat, we can see it as an opportunity: to cultivate trust, practice empathy, and expand the circle of meaningful connection. We begin to understand that being wrong is not the enemy—emotional isolation is.

Being open, curious, and willing to revise our views is not weakness—it is nourishment for the parts of us that truly hunger for connection and meaning.

What we need is trust in the world and in others, and trust in our own capacity to navigate uncertainty. When we have this, we can hold ambiguity with grace. We can say "I don't know" and not feel like the world is going to tumble down around us.

In other words, the real goal is not to be right. The real goal is to satisfy the deeper human needs that certainty superficially promises but cannot deliver: to feel safe in our impermanence, to feel trusted by others even when we falter, and to feel that our existence matters in a vast and mysterious world (for more of my thoughts on this, see chapter seven).

Intellectual vulnerability is a path to meeting that hunger authentically, without illusions. It's the slow, steady work of transforming the desire for certainty into the curiosity to explore, and the humility to connect.

Choosing Curiosity Over Certainty in Action

So how do we begin? In moments when our beliefs are challenged, we have options: double down and swing to the extreme, or—if we're willing—choose curiosity.

Here's what this looks like in daily life:

Workplace: Instead of dismissing a colleague's strategy, ask: "Can you walk me through your thinking?"

Social Media: Instead of firing back, pause: "What experiences might have shaped this person's perspective?"

Family: Instead of trying to win, sit down at the table asking questions, listening, and sharing humbly as if you, too, are on a journey of learning and exploring.

Small Practices:

- **Pause before responding.** When anyone shares an idea, or you encounter one online, notice your body's reaction. Before acting, wonder about what this means: what might this experience reveal about who you are, how you've been formed, and what matters to you?
- **Use "I" statements when you share:** "I think, I feel..."
- **Ask open questions**: "Help me understand..."
- **Share tentatively**: "From what I've read, it seems..."
- **Reflect afterward**: Journal, jot down in a notes app, or meditate on what surprised you.

Curiosity doesn't guarantee agreement, but it guarantees growth. It replaces the cheap thrill of being right with the deeper satisfaction of understanding, connection, and adaptability.

Exercises: Practicing Intellectual Vulnerability

Reflect on Certainty: Write down three beliefs you defend passionately. Ask: Why? What relationship do these beliefs have with your experiences of identity, belonging, and control?

Curiosity Pause: When challenged, pause and take a beat. Breathe. Can you genuinely listen without defending or going on the attack? Can you use this as an opportunity to learn about yourself or this other person?

Micro-Practice: Pick one belief this week. Notice your gut reaction at the thought of it being imperfect or having room for growth, then take a conscious step toward openness.

.

__Tip__: Certainty feels like safety, but it's curiosity that builds strength, resilience, and connection.

.

Recap & Reflection

Certainty is not an end-state to cherish. It is a cage. Today, each of us has the power—and, I daresay, the *responsibility*—to bust out and begin charting paths to greater connection, understanding, and freedom.

Why freedom, of all things? Because we didn't choose this. We might be comfortable in our cages, but we didn't stroll in with free and empowered intention. We darted in and locked the door behind us out of bare, even primal, survival instinct.

Now with awareness of the deeper needs for safety, peace, identity, and belonging driving this instinct, we can choose to do something else about it. We can step out, look around, and decide for ourselves. Maybe the right thing to do will ultimately be to turn around and go right back in the cage. But maybe it won't be. My hunch is that it won't be.

Freed from the drive to protect ourselves out of bare survival instinct, we can seek the things that really make us more safe: more understanding, more connection, more conversation, more open-hearted vulnerability, more trust in one another.

We can explore the great, wide-open sky of ideas more freely. We can do it alongside people who disagree with us, and welcome them as fellow seekers of truth.

Releasing certitude is not the end of our safety, peace, and joy. It is the beginning.

CHAPTER TWO

5 Signs You're in a Certainty Trap, and How to Get Out

In This Chapter, You Will...

-Uncover certainty traps—ordinary habits of mind that we all fall into when we cling too tightly to being right

-Explore five of the most common traps: defensiveness, black-and-white thinking, strong instinctive judgments, us/them dynamics, and victim mentality

-See how each of these traps creates an illusion of strength while actually narrowing the capacity for insight, connection, and growth

-Be able to identify when you're caught in a certainty trap—and begin shifting toward intellectual vulnerability instead

Five Traps that Inhibit Quality Thinking

Certainty traps protect our identity and soothe our anxieties, but they also wall us off from curiosity, dialogue, and growth. The more we fall prey to them, the more brittle our thinking becomes.

The five most common traps are defensiveness, black-and-white thinking, strong instinctive judgments, us/them dynamics, and victim mentality.

Let's examine these five traps one by one, starting with the most immediate and obvious.

Defensiveness

Defensiveness is usually the first sign you're caught in a trap. It shows up as a knee-jerk need to defend your beliefs, opinions, or competence—especially when they feel challenged.

Picture this: You're at a dinner party, and someone casually mentions they're thinking about switching to a plant-based diet. Before they can even explain why, you feel your chest tighten. "I could never do that," you hear yourself saying. "Humans need meat to be healthy. Our ancestors ate meat for thousands of years." The conversation shifts from a potential exchange of ideas into a debate where neither person is really listening.

In conversations, defensiveness often manifests as:
- Interrupting others to correct them immediately
- Feeling personally attacked by disagreement

- Lashing out to hurt someone who's hurt you, including unintentionally
- Turning discussions into arguments where the goal is to win, not learn

Defensiveness signals that someone has challenged a belief you use to hold yourself steady, likely one linked to your sense of identity, belonging, or control. While it's a natural human response, it blocks intellectual vulnerability. Every defensive reaction narrows your window of learning and strengthens the illusion that being correct is safer than being curious.

Think back to times you've felt your jaw tighten, your stomach knot, or your words sharpen when someone disagreed. That's your brain's alarm system signaling that your sense of safety is being tested. But here's the trap: these defensive reactions often exaggerate threat, magnify differences, and prevent learning. The more rigid your defenses, the more you reinforce your certainty—not your understanding.

Black-and-White Thinking: Good vs. Evil, Right vs. Wrong

Another common trap is black-and-white thinking. When we're caught in this pattern, we reduce complex issues to absolute categories:

- "People who disagree with me are stupid."
- "If you don't see it my way, you're evil."
- "Everything I believe is right; everything else is wrong."
- "You must fully support my cause or you're against it."

- "There's only one correct approach, and it's mine." Consider how this might play out at work: A colleague suggests a different approach to a project you've been leading. Instead of exploring the merits of their idea, black-and-white thinking kicks in: "They're trying to undermine my authority" or "They just don't understand the situation like I do." You dismiss their suggestion without genuinely considering whether it might improve the project. The conversation becomes adversarial rather than collaborative, and the project loses out on a potentially valuable perspective.

In politics, this can look, for example, like "the pro-life position is anti-feminist" or "the pro-choice position is anti-religious." These are over-simplifications that don't reflect the complexity of thought or depth of values of nearly anyone.

Such mental shortcuts provide a sense of safety—they reduce cognitive load and offer clear categories in a confusing world. They also strengthen group identity by creating clear boundaries between "us" and "them." But the cost is steep: black-and-white thinking prevents nuance, halts curiosity, and turns ordinary interactions into battles.

Life is rarely so neat, and the moment we begin to treat it as such, we create barriers to understanding ourselves and others.

Strong Instinctive Judgments

One of the clearest signals that you may be caught in a certainty trap is when you form immediate, strong judgments about people or ideas—whether positive or negative.

The Positive Trap

When you have an instant, intensely positive response to a person or idea—excitement, admiration, relief—you may be leaping to conclude they're "on your side" based on limited information. A single shared belief or cultural marker can trigger this response. From that moment, you'll tend to give them excessive benefit of the doubt, interpret their words with maximum charity, and eagerly incorporate their ideas into your worldview—even when careful consideration might reveal complexities you're overlooking.

The Negative Trap

The opposite happens with instant negative reactions—distaste, dismissal, or disgust. You may conclude they're "against you" based on superficial indicators. Then, their views get flattened into caricatures, their words scrutinized for flaws, their intentions dismissed, and you close yourself off from what they might genuinely offer.

Both reactions—celebratory and condemning—share the same problem: they shut down curiosity before it can begin. They represent your mind seeking the comfort of certainty rather than engaging with the complexity of reality. Strong instinctive judgments often signal premature closure rather than good discernment.

Us/Them Dynamics

When you see the world through an us-versus-them lens, complexity collapses into binaries: my side is right, your side is wrong; my tribe is virtuous, yours is corrupt.

Imagine scrolling through social media and seeing a post from someone with opposing political views. Instead of engaging with the content of their argument, us/them thinking immediately kicks in: "Of course they would say that—they're one of those people." The person becomes a representative of a category rather than an individual with their own experiences and reasoning.

While this mindset offers comfort by providing identity and belonging with clear anchors, it also shuts down curiosity and empathy. People who think differently are no longer individuals to understand—they become opponents to defeat, threats to your safety, and obstacles to your self-conception.

Us/them thinking fuels polarization, both on a cultural scale and in personal relationships. Its hallmarks include:

- Dismissing someone's argument because of who they seem to be rather than what they say
- Inflating the threat posed by those who disagree
- Feeling constantly under siege by the other side
- Viewing the other side as anti-truth or willfully ignorant

This pattern can appear in politics, academia, workplaces, and even friend groups. The more rigid the boundary, the less we grow, and the more our world narrows.

Victim Mentality: Righteousness as Armor

This subtle but perilous trap involves consistently framing yourself as righteous and under attack from others who are wrong, malicious, or ignorant. The signs include:

- Consistently believing that criticism or disagreement stems from others' moral failures or evil intent rather than legitimate differences of perspective
- Framing others' viewpoints as deliberate attacks on your character or group rather than honest expressions of their own experience
- Feeling justified in hostile responses because you perceive yourself as the innocent party defending against aggression

For example, when a coworker questions your proposal in a meeting, the victim mentality might incline you to interpret this as: "They're trying to make me look bad because they're threatened by my success" rather than considering that they might have genuine concerns or different insights.

Politically, the victim mentality can influence us subtly, as we can begin construing people on the other side as oppressors out to get us, not other humans who equally want the best for the world.

A victim mentality provides a sense of moral clarity and righteous purpose. It also deepens defensiveness, isolates you from feedback that could promote growth, and keeps you locked in your own perspective. When you're convinced you're always the wronged party, you lose the ability to examine your own contributions to conflict or to engage others as equals with valid experiences.

True intellectual vulnerability requires stepping down from the throne of persistent righteousness and engaging others as fellow imperfect humans trying to make sense of a complex world.

Of course, a victim mentality is different from recognizing actual harm or threat. Legitimate grievances deserve attention and action. What we're examining here is a persistent pattern of interpreting disagreement, criticism, or different perspectives as evidence of persecution.

Why These Are Traps

All five patterns—defensiveness, black-and-white thinking, strong instinctive reactions, us/them dynamics, and a victim mentality—share a common feature: they protect identity, belonging, and control at the expense of curiosity, learning, and connection.

Each trap offers the illusion of strength and safety. Defensiveness feels like protection. Black-and-white thinking feels like clarity. Strong judgments feel like discernment. Us/them dynamics feel like belonging. The victim mentality feels like righteousness.

But these are false strengths. They're psychological shortcuts that narrow our world rather than expand it. Like a fortress built on sand, they provide temporary shelter while making us more vulnerable in the long run. The walls we build to protect our certainties become the walls that imprison our growth.

Real strength comes from the ability to sit with uncertainty, to remain curious in the face of disagreement, and to see others as complex individuals rather than simple categories. This kind of strength isn't brittle—it's flexible, adaptive, and resilient.

Recognizing these traps as illusions of safety rather than sources of genuine security is the first step to dismantling them.

Exercise: Self-Assessment Quiz – "How Certain Are You?"

Take a few moments to reflect on your thinking habits. Answer each question honestly on a scale from 1 (not at all) to 5 (very much).

1. I feel uncomfortable when someone challenges my beliefs.
2. I often seek information that confirms what I already think.
3. I find it difficult to admit when I don't know something.
4. I prefer conversations where I "win" or prove my point.
5. I judge others quickly for holding different opinions.
6. I resist changing my mind, even when presented with new evidence.
7. I feel uneasy when I have to make decisions with incomplete information.

8. I label people or ideas as "right" or "wrong" rather than exploring nuances.

Scoring:
- **8–16:** You're likely comfortable with uncertainty and open to new ideas. Keep nurturing this openness.
- **17–28:** You may sometimes fall into certainty traps. The exercises in this chapter could help you build more intellectual flexibility.
- **29–40:** Certainty patterns may be significantly shaping your thinking. Consider this an opportunity for growth. The exercises that follow can help you develop new ways of engaging with uncertainty.

Remember, there's no shame in scoring high. We all fall into these traps; they're part of being human in a complex world.

Exercises: Spotting and Escaping Certainty Traps

1. Notice and Track Your Reactions

Throughout your day, especially when interacting with others or consuming media, pay attention to moments when you feel irritated, defensive, or dismissive. When you notice these feelings, take a breath and ask yourself:
- Am I thinking in terms of "us" versus "them"?
- Am I instantly dismissing someone or an idea without inquiry?

- Do I feel attacked, as if someone is threatening me, my values, and my vision for a safe future?

Make a mental note or jot down a quick reminder in your notes app. At the end of the day, reflect on these instances. Remember: this is a moment of self-awareness, not self-criticism.

2. Reframe the Situation

For each moment you identify, practice shifting your internal narrative:

- Replace "they are wrong/evil" with "they see the world differently—what might I learn from this?"
- Replace "I am being attacked" with "this is an opportunity to explore and understand, not to conquer or defend."
- Replace "I know better" with "we're both learning as we go."

Notice how shifting the internal narrative affects your emotional response.

3. Respond with Curiosity

People usually don't mean offense. When you notice defensiveness rising, try responding with genuine interest:

- "Help me understand what you mean by that."
- "Can you explain what led you to that perspective?"
- "What experiences shaped your thinking on this?"

- "How do you see this differently than I do?"

Even in disagreement, questions foster dialogue instead of debate.

4. Practice "I Don't Have the Complete Picture"

When you feel the pull to defend or assert certainty, try saying:
- "I'm not sure—I'd like to understand more."
- "I haven't explored that yet; can you help me see it?"
- "That's interesting. I see it differently, but I'm curious about your view."

You can practice this with others, or alone while reading or watching videos. Notice how this simple admission can transform tension into connection and open a path for mutual learning.

5. Reflect and Track Growth

At the end of the week, journal about these exercises:
- When did you notice a certainty trap?
- How did you respond differently?
- What new insights or understanding emerged?
- How did the shift affect your relationship or engagement?

Repeated practice trains the mind to pause before defensiveness kicks in, see others as collaborators rather than opponents, and embrace intellectual vulnerability as a strength.

Tip: *Three Signs You're Overly Certain*
- *Defensiveness pops up immediately* – You feel attacked or irritated when someone questions your beliefs.
- *You dismiss alternative perspectives* – You focus on proving yourself right rather than understanding others.
- *You struggle to say "I don't know"* – Admitting uncertainty feels risky or embarrassing.

Spotting these signs early helps you pause before rigidity sets in and creates space for curiosity and growth.

Recap & Reflection

Certainty traps are part of being human. They're reinforced by our culture, our fears, and our deep need for safety and belonging. But we can learn to recognize them and begin taking steps toward something better.

Moving from "I'm right, you're wrong" to "I think I'm right, but I'd love to hear what you think" represents a fundamental shift from domination to shared humanity.

Admitting you don't know something isn't shameful—it's courageous. It's the foundation of genuine learning, connection, and growth. When you say "I don't know" with intention and openness, you create space not just for your own growth, but for others to share their insights and experiences.

This is perhaps one of the most honorable things we can do: step out of our protective certainties and into a space where curiosity, humility, and mutual enrichment become possible.

CHAPTER THREE

The Life- and World-Changing Power of "I Don't Know"

In This Chapter, You Will...

-Follow my journey at Oxford, where saying "I don't know" in the face of brilliant peers taught me that admitting ignorance is a source of power, not shame

-Explore hidden benefits of admitting ignorance such as relief and camaraderie

-Learn techniques to transition from a culture of certainty to a culture of curiosity in your home, in classrooms, at work, and out in the world

The Night I Changed Everything at Oxford

I arrived at Oxford for my PhD in the fall of 2015 and instantly found myself surrounded by brilliant, intimidating people. After lectures or over pints at the pub, conversations swirled with philosophical jargon: terms like *biogenic structuralism* and *deontology* and *phenomenology*. It was usually assumed you just knew what all that meant.

One evening at the pub, standing in a circle of graduate students with drinks in hand, my dissertation supervisor used a term I'd never heard: Jacques Derrida's *carnophallogocentrism*. Everyone nodded sagely. At first, I stayed quiet. But I also knew that if I had any shot of meaningfully contributing to that conversation—which I really wanted to do—I first needed to know what the conversation was about.

I swallowed thickly and said: "I actually haven't read Derrida. Could you explain *carnophallogocentrism*?"

What happened next surprised me. Nearly everybody in that circle exhaled and exhibited other subtle signs of relief: grateful glances, small nods. It turned out I wasn't the only one who didn't know.

By admitting ignorance, I had given others permission to do the same—or at least, to breathe a little more easily under all that academic pressure and tweed. I was breathing easier too.

It also turns out I was right to ask. Once my supervisor explained that *carnophallogocentrism* refers to Derrida's critique of Western philosophy's interconnection between meat-eating, masculinity, and language, I saw a connection to something I had been wondering about theories of religion. I was able to mention it, then explore the connection more deeply with my supervisor later.

That moment revealed something profound: not knowing doesn't make you an imposter. It's the beginning of learning.

From Impostor to Expert Through Ignorance

That night changed how I approached my entire Oxford experience. I started going to seminars and shooting my hand into the air whenever I discerned an opportunity for growth. I got a bit of a reputation for it.

Many years after that night at the pub, I joined a seminar on analytic philosophy and the meaning of life. I was a total novice at analytic philosophy (a specific kind of philosophical analysis), and everyone else in the seminar was seasoned—some for decades. But within a few weeks I was positing original counterfactuals, a prized analytic tool, to the delight of everyone in that room.

I never would have learned the basics of analytic philosophy so quickly and been able to contribute meaningfully if I hadn't been so open about my ignorance at the beginning.

I thrived at Oxford not *in spite* of how much I said "I don't know," but *because* of it.

This experience taught me that intellectual vulnerability is one of the most powerful and reliable paths to growth. While we learn in other ways—through direct instruction, practice, observation—there's something uniquely effective about actively choosing to say "I don't know."

It doesn't just open the door to learning; it kicks it wide open.

How "I Don't Know" Transforms Everything

When we admit ignorance, we create conditions that make growth almost inevitable. We become genuinely curious. We listen more carefully. We ask better questions. We become receptive to information we might otherwise dismiss or overlook. We also empower others to do the same.

Ignorance is often seen as a deficit, something to hide. But in truth, "I don't know" is one of the most powerful sentences in any language. It opens social doors, builds trust, levels hierarchies, and forms the foundation of intellectual vulnerability.

We live in a culture that treats certainty as social capital. Usually, the more certain you seem (to both yourself and others), the more intelligence and expertise you seem to have. More people on your side also often adore you, because you're helping defend their views and making them feel safe. Your certainty helps give them confidence in their own certainty. But what do we unlock if we flip the script? What if we embrace our ignorance, celebrate our questions, and create a culture where it's curiosity—not certainty—that earns us esteem?

The Hidden Benefits of Admitting Ignorance

We tend to think of "I don't know" as weakness, but it unlocks benefits pretending to know never can:

Relief: Admitting you don't know stops the exhausting pretense. Think about the last time you sat in a meeting pretending to understand something you didn't—the mental energy required to maintain that façade is enormous. That honesty creates space to breathe and gives others permission to do the same.

Learning: Every skill, idea, and breakthrough starts in not knowing. When I admitted I didn't understand *carnophallogocentrism*, I gained access to a complex philosophical concept and made a meaningful connection to other ideas. Without that admission, I would have remained lost and unable to contribute.

Growth: Saying "I don't know" strengthens humility, flexibility, and resilience. Each admission is practice in being a learner rather than a performer. It trains you to face uncertainty without collapsing or hiding.

Better Solutions: We get stuck with suboptimal approaches to our health, relationships, careers, and self-talk whenever we cease being curious. "I don't have all the answers" is the first step to finding better ones.

Connection: Far from isolating you, "I don't know" draws people closer. It signals trust and invites solidarity. Others see themselves in your vulnerability, and conversations shift from posturing to more genuine exchange.

Building a Culture of Curiosity

We need a new culture: one that jettisons certainty and celebrates curiosity.

Some of the most promising examples we can look to for inspiration are innovation-focused environments. Here, admitting uncertainty is often recognized, or even celebrated, as essential to discovery. In these contexts, saying "I don't know" isn't seen as failure—it's the starting point for exploration. Bold hypotheses, experimentation, and productive failure are encouraged.

Imagine applying this innovative spirit to all areas of life: not just technological or scientific ideas, but also moral, spiritual, and political beliefs. All beliefs can be revised or updated to keep up with new happenings and learnings. We can constantly innovate our ideas.

Crucially, it's our most cherished beliefs—political, moral, and spiritual—that benefit most from revision. We tend to become more defensive and certainty-driven when ideas feel important to us. But we should be most eager to learn more when beliefs are so important and so much is at stake.

Modeling Curiosity for the Next Generation

This cultural shift becomes especially important when we consider how we're teaching young people. Children are naturally curious, but that curiosity can get discouraged as they learn to navigate social expectations and performance pressures.

When adults proudly say "I don't know," they show kids that not having the answer isn't shameful—it's the starting point of intellectual adventure. The discomfort of doubt or of being judged pushes us to rush to "I know." But holding ourselves back from that relief and sitting in uncertainty expands the time we can spend exploring and discovering.

The philosopher John Dewey once said that the ability to "sit in doubt" may be the most important attribute teachers can impart to their students. When children learn to honor doubt and explore their ignorance and questions, they learn to suspend the comforts of certainty long enough to test ideas, imagine alternatives, and discover new truths.

If children see parents, teachers, and mentors approach the unknown with openness instead of shame, they learn that curiosity is something to cultivate, not hide. Doubt becomes less uncomfortable and more of a sign that adventure is afoot.

Each admission of not-knowing is a gift to others, especially kids: it teaches that learning is a journey rather than a performance of mastery.

Exercises: Practicing "I Don't Know"

Personal Practice

Name Your Unknowns: List three areas where you feel you should or could know more. Write one question you genuinely want to explore but have avoided asking. Consider including policy positions you consider opposite to yours, such as, for example, "Pro-Choice" or "Pro-Life." Also consider including your own cherished beliefs, as sometimes there are important unknowns in our own positions. For example, I identified as "Pro-Choice" for a long time before I even thought to examine the legal and scientific arguments concerning it.

Admit It Out Loud: In a safe setting, say: "I don't know, could you explain?" Notice the emotions that arise—fear, embarrassment, relief, curiosity—and record your observations.

Observe Group Dynamics: Notice how others admit or hide ignorance in discussions. How does it affect tone, engagement, and your own responses? Try creating moments of shared not-knowing.

Celebrate It: End a day or week by reflecting on one time you admitted not knowing. Note the relief, learning, growth, or connection it brought.

Teaching Curiosity to Others

Spur-of-the-Moment Questions:

When asked a question you can't immediately answer, resist guessing. Say, "I don't know—but let's find out."
- Brainstorm possible answers together
- Look for resources—books, trusted websites, or other experts
- Reflect together on surprises and lessons from the process
- The aim is making uncertainty safe and exploration joyful

The "Curiosity Board" (for classrooms or teams):
- Dedicate a space where people can post unanswered questions
- Weekly, explore one or two questions together, beginning with open-ended brainstorming
- Rotate responsibility so different people guide the "let's find out" process
- Emphasize that value lies in exploration and teamwork as much as answers

Family "Wonder Rounds":
- Invite everyone to share one thing they wondered about that day
- Allow space for speculation, storytelling, or connections to lived experience
- Later, research answers together or assign someone to report back
- This turns doubt into a ritual of connection and reinforces curiosity as a shared value

Recap & Reflection

Saying "I don't know" is not weakness—it's wisdom. It signals honesty, creates space for learning, and draws people together. The cultural script tells us to bluff, posture, and perform—but we have the power to rewrite it.

That rewriting begins with recognizing a simple truth: the fertile ground in which discovery grows isn't the soil of certainty—it's the honest admission that we still have more to learn. Every time we choose curiosity over performance, we plant seeds that can grow into understanding, connection, and genuine expertise.

What do we unlock when we choose to be innovators of our *minds?*

CHAPTER FOUR

10 Ways to Choose Growth Over Being Right

In This Chapter, You Will...

-Discover practical ways to strengthen your intellectual vulnerability, learning to hold your beliefs with curiosity, humility, and openness

-Practice noticing when your convictions or identity are constraining your growth

-Cultivate delight in being wrong

-Learn to pause, probe, and respond with curiosity and respect, transforming every interaction into a chance to grow, connect, and thrive

The Mental Gym of Intellectual Vulnerability

Intellectual vulnerability is not easy at first for most. But with practice, just like any other habit, it becomes more natural over time.

Think of intellectual vulnerability as a kind of mental gym. Just as our bodies grow stronger through stretching, lifting, and balancing, our minds grow stronger through questioning, pausing, and listening. Every moment of friction—when we feel defensive, offended, or certain we're right—is like a weight we can choose to pick up. The more we practice lifting these moments with patience and curiosity, the more resilient and flexible we become.

This chapter offers practical tools for building that strength. Instead of measuring ourselves by how firmly we defend our beliefs, we can measure by how generously we question, how attentively we listen, and how courageously we say, "I don't know."

The aim is not perfection but progress—learning to pause, to reframe, and to treat others as fellow travelers on the way. With practice, the mental gym of intellectual vulnerability doesn't just make us stronger; it makes us more connected, more alive, and more human.

1. Switch from Focusing on *What* You Believe to *How*

Most of us build friendships and communities based on shared beliefs. But what if we build relationships based on being able to safely share and explore beliefs together? What happens when you no longer need friends to agree with you, but can talk warmly whether you agree or not?

When you focus on *how* you believe—with humility, curiosity, and a genuine desire to revise as you learn from others—rather than just *what* you believe, several things become possible:

- You can maintain meaningful friendships with people across the belief spectrum
- Your relationships reach new levels of trust and authenticity
- Your ideas improve because your "how" commits you to ongoing learning and growth
- You gain perspective across all areas of life in surprising ways

2. Identify as "On The Way"

Many anchor themselves in ideological identities: "I'm a conservative," "I'm a progressive," "I'm a feminist," "I'm an ally of X," etc. These labels offer belonging, clarity, and a sense of control—but they can trap us.

When we fuse our self-concept with rigid ideological positions:
- Our minds close to learning from those who disagree or simply refuse the labels
- Nuance feels threatening; compromise seems like betrayal
- Growth stalls, as changing a belief can feel like losing a part of ourselves

What if we shifted focus from positions to processes? Instead of primarily identifying as "conservative" or "progressive," you could, as I do, say:
- "I'm a learner."
- "I'm growth-oriented."
- "I'm on the way."

Process-based identities don't demand abandoning values—they allow us to hold them lightly while remaining open to evidence, perspectives, and experiences. They let curiosity, humility, and reflection become core to our self-concept, in addition to, or in place of, beliefs we defend.

Certainty may feel safe, but process-based curiosity builds resilience, adaptability, and connection. It frees us to:
- Listen without defensiveness
- Engage without hostility
- Learn publicly without fear of losing ourselves

Imagine how differently you might approach a heated discussion if your primary identity was "learner" rather than "conservative" or "progressive." The position-holder asks: "How can I defend this?" The learner asks: "What can this teach me?"

3. Respect Others as Fellow Travelers

Every person is a world of experiences, biases, and partial truths. Just as your understanding is evolving, so is theirs. When we see others as fellow travelers rather than opponents or obstacles, we can:

- Avoid labeling them as wrong, stupid, or immoral
- Assume their intentions are reasonable, even if their conclusions seem misguided
- Honor the limits of their knowledge—and your own
- Stay curious about how they arrived at their beliefs

This doesn't mean accepting harmful ideas or abandoning your values. It means recognizing that most people are doing their best to make sense of the world with the information and experiences they have. Respecting others as fellow travelers strengthens trust, creates space for dialogue, and models the curiosity you hope to cultivate.

We only learn through encounters with difference. Often, it is the people most different from us who have the most to teach us.

Other people may not be all correct, but we're not either. None of us are fully intellectually complete. We're all fellow travelers, and we can celebrate one another as sources of insight and growth.

4. Change Your Goal from *Be Correct* to *Broaden and Deepen Understanding*

Be correct is limited and stops once you establish "correctness." *Broaden and deepen understanding* is a never-ending quest that expands your mind endlessly.

Even the simplest claims about reality can be unpacked and explored without end. Consider a simple example: "Blueberries are blue."

Are they? I'm not so sure. That depends on how you define the terms "blueberry" and "blue." Doing that is a lot more complex than it can seem at first glance.

What does "blue" mean? How does the human ability to see a limited frequency range of electromagnetic waves influence what we see, or don't see? And do we all see the same colors, and how do color definitions vary across cultures, and where do we draw the lines between blue and different colors, and what about color blindness, and partial blindness?

What does "blueberry" mean? How many species of blueberry are there, and are they all the same shade of "blue," or do they differ from one another, or across different stages of ripeness, or across different climates, and are any of them genetically engineered, and how has that influenced them, and how have they evolved since humans began mass producing them, and what is a species anyway?

Understanding of "blue" and "blueberries" could be broadened and deepened forever.

The same applies to other people, other belief systems, other political visions.

By seeking greater understanding, as opposed to just being "right," you open yourself to keep learning forever.

5. Ask Socratic Questions of Others (and Yourself)

Socratic questioning means asking people about their ideas. This helps them understand their own arguments better while also potentially illuminating gaps. It is a powerful tool. It's not about "trapping" someone or proving them wrong—even though some people, including Socrates, occasionally use it like that! It's about digging deeper, uncovering assumptions, and widening understanding. Pause and ask questions like:

- What do you mean by that?
- How are you defining that term?
- Have you considered the impact of this other phenomenon on what you're suggesting?
- How do you envision this playing out in real life?

You can also turn these questions toward yourself. Pause and wonder: What do I mean by that? How am I defining that term? Have I fully explored the implications of this idea?

You may be amazed by what you find.

Socratic questioning invites curiosity and mutual learning. It turns all dialogues—external or internal—into explorations instead of battles.

6. Seek Mutual Enrichment Rather than Victory

Most people enter conversations trying to prove they're right—to win. Winning provides a temporary high of safety and superiority, but it's ultimately isolating.

Mutual enrichment invites different intentions:

- Offering your perspective as a gift, not a weapon
- Listening to understand, not to find flaws
- Seeing disagreement as an opportunity for both people to grow

You don't have to change this person in any specific way for the conversation to be a success. I invite your curiosity: what does success mean to you? To me, success means growth for both parties.

For your conversation partner, enrichment means learning and increasing understanding (whether that means moving closer to your own position or not). How can you help them on their journey toward truth? You can ask Socratic questions and offer your ideas hoping to spark something inside them. These things are enriching and contribute to deeper musings, even if you don't see obvious movement or change on the surface in that moment.

In turn, you can seek to learn. You can ask questions to learn about what it means to be them, why they are the way they are, and why they think the way they think. You can listen to what they say and try to understand where they're coming from.

When you seek to learn, you also create the side benefit of empowering your conversation partner to think more clearly because it makes them feel more respected.

Consider the difference:

- **Victory mindset:** "I need to show them they're wrong about climate change."
- **Mutual enrichment mindset:** "I wonder what experiences have shaped their perspective on environmental issues. Maybe I can share what's influenced my thinking and learn about theirs."

7. Cultivate Delight in Being Wrong

Many of us have been trained to fear mistakes. Intellectual vulnerability flips the script: being wrong is a gift. Finding out you're wrong:

- Highlights gaps in knowledge
- Enables you to find new solutions to old problems
- Can spark curiosity and exploration
- Can be a moment of humility, connection, and growth

Instead of embarrassment or shame, discover a sense of pride and purpose in saying, "I was wrong—here's what I learned."

"I'm *on the way.*"

8. Transform Friction and Conflict into Opportunities to Learn

Friction and conflict are inevitable, but they don't have to be destructive. Any feeling of offense, anger, or defensiveness signals that something important is happening inside you. Some idea central to your identity, belonging, or control feels threatened.

But feeling attacked and being attacked are different things. And even if your beliefs genuinely are being challenged, fighting isn't your only option.

When you feel activated in conversation, pause and ask:

- What does this reveal about my assumptions or triggers?
- What might the other person be reacting to in me?
- Can this become an opportunity to explore rather than escalate?
- What can I learn about myself from this emotional response?
- What can I learn about them?

Every strong reaction in conversation provides data. Curiosity about that data can transform potential conflict into mutual learning.

For instance, if someone's response to a belief you've stated makes you defensive, instead of attacking back, you might pause and think: "Why did that hit me so hard? What am I afraid they're seeing? What might they actually be trying to communicate?"

To be clear: in this moment of pausing, discernment is crucial. You might conclude the attack and potential for harm are real. If so, excuse yourself. There's no point in engaging in a destructive conversation.

9. Set Healthy Boundaries

Intellectual vulnerability does not mean tolerating abuse or disrespect. Boundaries matter:

- Step away from conversations that are hostile or unsafe
- Protect your mental and emotional energy
- Model respectful dialogue while honoring your limits

You can explain as much or as little about why you are excusing yourself as you like.

Boundaries are not a failure of vulnerability—they're a safeguard that makes sustained intellectual openness possible.

10. Question Yourself More Than Questioning Others

Many people pride themselves on being skeptical of others' claims. But this approach has a hidden flaw: we typically apply skepticism selectively, questioning those we already disagree with while giving free passes to those who confirm our existing beliefs.

This selective skepticism leads us deeper down familiar paths rather than opening us to new territory.

For each of us, the greatest obstacle to truth isn't other people—it's the limitations of our own experience. We've each only seen the world through 1/8000000000th of the total human perspective. There's a greater chance we're held back by attachment to what we presently see and think than by being open to the 7,999,999,999 people out there on other mountaintops seeing and thinking other things.

We're all sure of what we know, but that's only because of what we've been through. The path to learning is knocking ourselves out of tunnel vision. It's turning that questioning gaze inward at ourselves.

Ask yourself:

- What has shaped my perspective on this issue?
- Why am I drawn to certain arguments and repelled by others?
- What experiences make me friendly toward some people and beliefs but not others?
- What perspectives might I be missing that could add nuance, depth, or breadth to my understanding?

Daily Practices: Building Your Intellectual Vulnerability Muscle

These principles become habits through consistent small practices:

Morning Curiosity Check: Start each day by identifying one belief you hold strongly. Write down one genuine question about it.

Conversation Experiment: In one discussion today, challenge yourself to ask only questions—no assertions, no rebuttals, just curious exploration.

Evening Reflection: Before bed, note one moment when you discovered you were wrong about something small. What did it teach you?

Find the Delight in Being Wrong: Note one moment each day when you discovered you were wrong. Reflect on what it taught you. Celebrate that learning. Try doing this with family members or friends to build a culture of curiosity.

Weekly Perspective Hunt: Seek out one person this week who sees the world differently than you do. Listen with genuine curiosity about their experience.

Friction Journal: When you feel defensive or triggered, pause and write, or make a note to revisit later: "What is this teaching me about myself?"

- **Tip**: *Three Questions to Ask Before You Argue*
    1. Am I seeking understanding or victory?
    2. Could my certainty be limiting my growth?
    3. How can I contribute curiosity and respect here?

    These three questions act as a mental reset. They shift your orientation from combat to exploration, from defensiveness to curiosity, and from rigidity to openness.

-

Recap & Reflection

Intellectual vulnerability isn't weakness—it's the strength to stay open, humble, and curious in a world that prizes certainty. Each practice in this chapter reminds us that being on the way is more rewarding than winning and that dialogue enriches us more than debate.

With time, these habits reshape not only how we think but how we connect with others. They deepen trust, expand compassion, and build resilience against the brittleness that comes from clinging too tightly to being right.

By choosing curiosity over rigidity and growth over victory, you create a life where every conversation becomes an opportunity to learn, to enrich yourself and others, and to flourish in ways you never expected.

CHAPTER FIVE

How to Talk Across Any Divide: A Practical Guide

> In This Chapter, You Will...
>
> -Learn practical ways to pause, listen, share, and repair, transforming potentially tense conversations into opportunities for understanding
>
> -Discover how to zoom out to find shared values, so that differences deepen connection instead of driving it apart
>
> -Become equipped to have mutually enriching conversation with any other well-intentioned person, no matter the chasm in your beliefs

When Good Friends Face Political Division

My friend Robert came to one of our biweekly coffee dates in an unusual state of distress. He sat down, removed his hat, and confessed:

"I think the men's group is falling apart."

Ah. Got it. This would distress anyone who knew Robert. The Men's Group—eight close friends who gather for retreats and regular meetings—has been one of the greatest sources of joy in Robert's life. These men love each other deeply. I've been moved to tears listening to tales of their connection and fraternity.

But recently, they've discovered they disagree politically. *Uh oh.* Most lean liberal, but a few, including one of Robert's closest friends, have been exploring more conservative views. This friend isn't trying to fight—he's looking for understanding and acceptance. But when his thoughts meet crossed arms instead of nods, he feels excluded. Sometimes others in the group respond with frustration. Robert feels defensive, though he doesn't want to, while others threaten to leave if politics come up at all.

Now they're wondering: *can we survive as friends?*

This story isn't unique. Tragically, it's become commonplace for political differences to end relationships that once thrived on mutual respect, care, and love.

The Real Problem Isn't Disagreement—It's Distrust

We often assume our social divisions stem from disagreement itself, but that's not quite right. Disagreement is natural, even healthy. In the mid- and late-1900s, some prominent scholars worried the US wasn't polarized enough—that too much consensus was stifling democratic debate.

In reality, Americans' positions on core policy issues haven't shifted dramatically. What has changed is our perception of the "other side." We imagine they are extreme, hostile, and immoral. As a result, they cannot be trusted.

In 2016, the majority of people in both political parties in the USA expressed not just unfavorable but "very unfavorable" views of the other party for the first time since these surveys began. By 2022, Americans had become almost twice as likely to describe people in the other party as immoral and dishonest compared to 2016. Large majorities in both parties also described the other party as more close-minded than other Americans.

But here's the crucial question: What do we really need to preserve democracy and build a better society? Is it to villainize, oversimplify, and fight with one another? Or might it be empathizing, engaging, and working with one another?

The rest of this chapter offers practical tools for choosing the second path—for rebuilding trust and learning to talk across difference.

Start with the Right Foundation: Benefit of the Doubt

Most people genuinely believe they're pursuing truth and doing what's right. I have never met a single person who doesn't hold truth as one of their highest values. What about you?

It seems to me that we all value truth highly; we just see it differently and have different ideas about what will create a safe and just future. We've been exposed to different concepts and gone through different experiences. Of course we're going to have different ideas about what will make the world the safest, most ethical, and most just place.

We've been trained to see these differences as threats, but we can treat them as opportunities. What am I missing because of how my own life has been limited? I have no idea. But I'm eager to keep finding out.

The vast majority of people don't mean harm. They want the world to thrive every bit as much as you do. Of course, some people genuinely do mean harm. If you're in a situation that feels potentially dangerous, remove yourself. Set boundaries. Loving others doesn't mean subjecting yourself to abuse.

But most of the time, even when words sting, it's not malicious. People are usually acting from sincere convictions, past experiences, insecurities, and attempts to navigate a complicated world—just like you are.

What if, before leaping to conclusions and erecting barriers, we paused and got curious about what was happening between us?

Set Yourself Up for Success

Before stepping into a potentially difficult conversation, preparation can matter as much or more than what you say. Here's how to create conditions for genuine dialogue:

Check your own readiness

Ask yourself: "Am I calm enough to listen? Am I available for connection?" If you're angry or itching for a fight, wait. Beginning a hard conversation when you're already activated almost guarantees escalation.

Be clear about your intent

Don't leave your motives unclear, especially if there's been prior conflict. Signal openness from the start: "I want to understand your perspective, not fight to win," or "I'm hoping we can explore this together." These simple statements lower defenses and makes real listening possible.

Establish simple ground rules

Consider agreeing on basic boundaries: "Let's both commit to listening fully before responding," or "If either of us feels too heated, let's pause and return later."

You can set these boundaries internally even if you don't discuss them explicitly.

Signal care explicitly

Don't assume the other person knows you value them. Say it directly: "Our relationship matters more to me than agreement," or "I care about you even when we see things differently." Care is the foundation that makes difficult conversations safe.

When you enter a hard conversation this way—with readiness, clear intent, appropriate boundaries, and explicit care—you shift the tone from adversarial to collaborative.

How to Pause for Insight and Empowerment

Feeling attacked and being attacked are not the same thing. A pause creates space to notice emotions and reflect on what's really happening—both within you and the other person.

When you feel your defenses rising, try asking:
- What is my defensive reaction revealing about my sense of identity, belonging, or control?
- What might this person's words reveal about theirs?

- Could there be another way to interpret what just happened?

Like any skill, pausing strengthens with practice. At first, it may feel awkward, but over time, it becomes a reflex that protects relationships instead of escalating conflict.

Simple Pause Techniques

- Count to ten slowly before responding
- Silently label what you're feeling: "I feel attacked," "I feel angry," "I feel misunderstood"
- Ask yourself: "What else could be true about why they said this?"
- Notice physical sensations—tight jaw, clenched fists, shallow breathing
- Remind yourself reactions come from pain and fear; what you do about that is up to you

This skill applies whether you're in conversation with someone or consuming content by youreslf. Pay attention to your inner landscape and pause when you feel yourself beginning to react emotionally.

How to Listen to Build Bridges

Curiosity can be seen as an attitude of intellectual exploration and play, but in a hard conversation, curiosity can benefit from structure. Simply telling yourself to "be curious" usually isn't enough.

Here are some ways to listen that proactively encourage the other person to open up:

Reflect back

One of the simplest and most effective listening practices is to mirror back what you think you've heard: "What I hear you saying is..."

Then, it's usually good to end on a question: "Am I getting that right?"

This isn't parroting—it's offering a respectful summary in your own words. Done well, it shows the other person that they've been heard, lowers defensiveness, and gives them the chance to clarify if you've misunderstood.

Don't say: "That's ridiculous. You're saying the government is always wrong?"

Do say: "So it sounds like you're worried the government doesn't have our best interests in mind. Did I hear you right?"

Honor deeper values

Beneath most stances lie deeper values—of freedom, safety, fairness, dignity, belonging. Surfacing these is powerful. It doesn't just show you care, but also enables you both to feel connected over shared concerns.

You might say: "It sounds like safety is really important to you. Did I get that right?" or "It seems like freedom matters most to you here."

By naming values, you acknowledge the person's humanity, not just their opinion. Even if you disagree with their conclusion, you're affirming something deeper you can both respect.

Don't say: "That's just fear talking."

Do say: "It sounds like safety is really important to you in this conversation. I can understand why. Is that correct?"

Listen for story, not just stance

Arguments often calcify when we only trade positions. Asking how someone came to hold their beliefs invites movement and facilitates understanding: "Can you tell me a bit about how you came to feel this way?" or "Was there a specific experience that shaped how you see this issue?"

Stories soften the edges of certainty. They reintroduce nuance, history, and vulnerability—and they allow us to see the person, not just the platform.

Don't say: "You're just wrong—end of story."

Do say: "I'm curious, was there a particular experience that shaped how you came to this view?"

When you listen in these ways, you're not giving anything up—you're widening the space in which truth can grow.

Reflective listening affirms, values-based listening dignifies, and story-based listening humanizes. Together, they turn conversations that might divide into opportunities to connect.

How to Share Without Escalating

Listening builds a bridge, but eventually you'll need to walk across it and share your own perspective. The challenge is to do so without setting off alarms of defensiveness or attack.

Three practices help: speaking from your own experience (using "I" language), leading with values, and being clear about the difference between your story and a universal claim.

Use I-language instead of you-language

Framing your words from your own perspective softens their impact and reduces blame.

Don't say: "You're wrong about this."

Do say: "I've struggled to make sense of this issue, and here's how I see it right now."

That subtle shift makes your words less of a verdict and more of an offering. It signals openness instead of judgment.

Lead with values and experiences before positions

People connect more easily with what you care about and what you've lived through than with policy positions or abstract conclusions.

Try beginning with what matters to you: "I care a lot about fairness, and my own experience in healthcare has shaped how I think about this policy." By grounding your stance in shared human concerns—safety, dignity, justice—you create the possibility of resonance, even across disagreement.

Don't say: "The only logical stance is mine."

Do say: "Because I've seen loved ones struggle in the system, protection for this set of circumstances feels especially urgent to me here."

Distinguish personal story from universal claim

When you share your experience, resist the temptation to make it definitive for everyone. Story invites openness; universals forge resistance.

Saying "In my family, masks felt like protection during the pandemic" leaves space for someone else's experience to differ. Saying "Masks are always the right choice, no matter what" shuts that door.

Don't say: "Anyone who disagrees with me is blind to reality."

Do say: "In my own life, this has been the reality—and it's why I care so much about it."

Speaking this way doesn't weaken your convictions; it strengthens their credibility. The goal is not to win, but to stay in the conversation long enough for something new to emerge.

How to Repair After Rupture

Even with the best preparation and the gentlest intentions, conversations sometimes still break down.

Many people avoid difficult dialogue altogether because they fear rupture. But rupture does not have to be the end of the story—it can be an ordinary, even important, part of human relationship. What matters most is whether you try to repair.

Three guidelines:

Acknowledge the rift directly

When things go badly, name it. This isn't weakness; it's honesty. Owning your part lowers the temperature and signals maturity.

Don't: Pretend nothing happened. ("So, anyway, what's for dinner?")

Do: Say, "That conversation was hard. I know I didn't listen as well as I wanted to."

By stepping forward first, you create a pathway for the other person to step forward too.

Reaffirm the relationship

After conflict, people often worry: Are we still okay? Offering reassurance keeps connection intact even when agreement feels impossible.

Don't: Withdraw in silence. ("If they don't text me first, I won't bother.")

Do: Say, "Even when we disagree, you matter to me."

That reminder makes it safer to come back together later.

Invite re-engagement later

Sometimes the most productive move is not to push through in the heat of the moment, but to pause and return when both parties can breathe.

Don't: Slam the door. ("I can't talk to you about this ever again.")

Do: Say, "Could we try again another time? I want to keep working on this with you."

This simple gesture communicates hope—that the conversation, and the relationship, are worth another chance.

Repair is what gives people the courage to risk real conversations in the first place. Knowing that mistakes are survivable—that you can stumble and still find your way back—turns intellectual vulnerability from an intellectual posture into an interpersonal bridge that brings you closer.

Zoom Out to Find Common Ground

When disagreements feel intense, you can step back and look for shared values. Freedom, safety, health, justice, education, art, wisdom, truth, and well-being are a few core values that unite us far more than the particulars divide us.

Conflicts often arise not from lack of care about these values, but from differing ideas about how best to honor them.

Don't: Get stuck in the weeds of disagreement. When the details feel overwhelming or emotions run high, it's easy to fixate on positions: who's right, who's wrong, and whose facts are stronger. This narrow focus often makes us double down and miss what truly matters.

Do: Step back and ask: What deeper values are we both trying to protect?

Example: Instead of "You're wrong about healthcare policy," try, "It sounds like we both care about people being healthy and secure. We just have different ideas about how to get there." Naming the shared value reframes the conversation from combat to collaboration.

Don't: Assume the worst about intentions. Believing the other person is driven by malice or ignorance obscures common ground and keeps both of you defensive.

Do: Test for shared goals by asking open questions: "What do we both want in the long run?" or "What concern is most important to you here?" These questions shift the energy from argument to discovery, reminding you that both sides are trying to protect something precious.

Example: If a friend insists on stricter security policies, you might respond, "It sounds like safety is really important to you. That matters to me, too—I just worry about protecting freedom at the same time." Now you're not adversaries—you're partners in weighing values.

When you zoom out to shared commitments, you transform tension into learning. The conversation no longer has to end in "agreement" to be meaningful; instead, it becomes a way to deepen understanding, challenge assumptions, and refine your own thinking.

The Men's Group Survives

Remember Robert and his men's group facing political division? The tools in this chapter have been a part of their moving forward. Instead of avoiding political topics or demanding agreement, the group recommitted or began to:
- Start with explicit affirmation of their care for each other
- Establish ground rules for political conversations
- Practice listening for the values behind different positions
- Share personal experiences rather than abstract arguments
- Repair quickly when conversations get heated
- Remember that their friendship matters more than political agreement, even when political differences feel very important

Change hasn't been overnight. But they're still friends. They're still talking it all through. They're charting their path ahead, together.

The goal isn't to eliminate disagreement but to disagree well—with curiosity, respect, and genuine care for each other's humanity.

Recap & Reflection

There's a larger promise here. Every time you choose trust over suspicion, learning over certainty, and connection over division (while setting healthy boundaries), you don't just preserve individual relationships—you practice the skills our democracy desperately needs.

You model what it looks like to engage difference with wisdom and grace. You prove that it's possible to care deeply about important issues while treating others with dignity and respect.

In a world full of people convinced that those who disagree with them are enemies, choosing to see others as fellow travelers seeking truth is both radical and essential.

The future of our communities—and perhaps our society—may well depend on enough people learning to talk across divides with the kind of wisdom, patience, and hope these tools can unlock.

CHAPTER SIX

The Gift of Re-Imagining Truth as Imperfect & On The Way

In This Chapter, You Will...

-Free yourself from cultural assumptions about what it means to be true

-Explore a new way of thinking about truth—not as a fixed point, but as a journey that unfolds over time

-Begin holding your beliefs lightly, engaging with uncertainty, and seeing every idea as a provisional step toward deeper understanding

-Become equipped to treat truth as "on the way," transforming each belief, conversation, and moment of doubt into an opportunity for learning, growth, and connection

The Problem with How We Think About Truth

Picture this scenario: You're at a dinner party, and someone makes a confident statement about climate change, education policy, or the best way to raise children. Within minutes, the conversation has devolved into a heated argument where people are defending their positions as if their lives depend on it.

Many in the room begin accusing one another of failing to see the real truth of things. One person says loudly, sounding frustrated: "How can you deny this reality?"

Some others try to end the conflict by asserting there's no real truth. One says: "Well that's *your* truth and this is *my* truth, and that's all there is to it!"

Why do both these things happen so often? Why do we shout at one another about who's right? Or why do we sometimes throw our hands up and say it's impossible?

There are many reasons for this, but one deeply buried and important one is that we have, as a society, inherited a problematic way of thinking about truth: it must be perfect. We assume that a true statement has to be perfectly true or it's got no truth at all.

This wedges us between the rock and hard places of "I'm right" and "Nobody can be right."

The two views are:

Absolute Certainty: Truth is perfect, and knowable, and you're the one who's got it.

- "I know the truth completely, and anyone who disagrees is wrong."

Pure Relativism: Truth claims must be perfect, but they *can't* be, so there's no way to make truth claims.

- "It's impossible to say for sure, so no perspective is better than any other."

Both approaches create problems. The first leads to rigid certainty and endless arguments. The second excuses misinformation and moral indifference. Neither captures the nature of truth or how learning actually works in real life.

What if there's a third way?

Truth Is a Journey, Not a Destination

After researching this problem for a decade and reading a lot of under-appreciated philosophers with under-appreciated ideas, I offer a new way to think about truth:

Truth is real, but it's also always developing. It's being gained, imperfectly, over time. It's *on the way*.

In the introduction I explained that I think about beliefs as maps of reality. Each of us draws our own map of reality while standing on one mountaintop, glimpsing the territory of reality through our own grimy binoculars. We *do* see the actual territory—just imperfectly.

People who embrace the Absolute Certainty view of truth believe their maps are perfect. When others (rightly) push back against this, they usually end up advocating for Pure Relativism because they don't see another way. They end up saying, even if they dislike it: "Get off your rocker. None of our maps can match."

I offer a third, middle way. Instead of running all the way to "our maps can't match at all" with the Pure Relativists, we can respond to the Absolute Certaintists saying: "Yes, your map matches reality a little bit and so does mine. All our maps match at least a little, but they're all imperfect, partial, and incomplete."

We can know things about reality—we have to, or we wouldn't survive—but our knowledge, as both individuals and societies, is always incomplete and generally improving, imperfectly and unevenly.

Truth is on the way. Improving the scope and granularity of maps takes time. **Truth is literally a journey, not a destination.**

Consider the arc of human history. When the human species first evolved into being hundreds of thousand years ago, how much did we know? At the very beginning, there was zero knowledge. Today, there is a lot! In between, there has been an enormous amount of observation, experimentation, revision, etc: imperfectly broadening and deepening insight into reality over time.

Consider the arc of your own life. How have you come to know everything you know? Did you go to school, study things other people discovered and researched, then go out into the world and experience what you experienced? Did all this not require learning, and therefore time?

Have you not been revising your thoughts all along?

Think about something you believed strongly five years ago that you now see differently. Maybe it's about parenting, politics, health, or relationships. Did you abandon the truth when you changed your mind, or did you get closer to it?

I often wonder: *what am I missing? What are we, together as a species, missing? How can we explore more of what we seem to know today to know more tomorrow?*

To me, the most thrilling question of the present moment isn't *what have we learned so far?* But *what do we have yet to learn?*

We literally cannot imagine it.

This is what I mean by "truth on the way": knowledge is real and valuable but also provisional and evolving.

How Science Shows Us Truth Evolves

Scientific progress provides clear examples of how truth develops over time without invalidating past truth.

When Charles Darwin published *On the Origin of Species* in 1859, he so thoroughly revolutionized the understanding of life he blew everybody's minds. His insights about natural selection had a lot of truth. But Darwin didn't understand how traits were inherited. He knew that offspring resembled parents but couldn't explain the mechanism.

It wasn't until Gregor Mendel published insights from his work with pea plants in the following decade that patterns of inheritance were incorporated into the study of evolution and genetics.

Then, it wasn't until the discovery of the double helix structure of DNA in the 1950s that we actually learned the molecular chemistry of how genes get passed down.

After that, there have continued to be both major and minor refinements to evolutionary theory.

Was Darwin wrong because his theory was incomplete? Of course not. His insights remain foundational. But our understanding has grown more comprehensive, more accurate, more useful. I think of this in terms of having *more truth*. Darwin's theory *had* truth then, though today, collectively, our understanding *has relatively more*.

Or consider physics. Many people debate the validity of Newton's laws of motion. In 1687, Newton's book *Principia Mathematica* revolutionized the scientific community's understanding of mass, energy, gravity, and force. Today, we understand that Newton's laws work perfectly well for everyday objects, but they break down in the realms of the very large and very small. To accurately describe motion of very large or very small bodies, you need Einstein's relativity and quantum mechanics respectively. Was Newton "right"? To me, that's not a great question. A better question is: *How much insight into reality did Newton have?* The answer is: *Some. But today, we have more.*

Ideas can even have significant inaccuracies but still some amount of truth. For example, until about 150 years ago, the most esteemed scientific and medical authorities in the West believed disease came from what they called *miasma*: toxic vapors from rotting organic matter. The theory was not accurate, but they knew that rotting food was highly toxic, so this was a kernel of truth in the flawed theory. This kernel ultimately helped carry their thinking forward. The highly imperfect *miasma* hypothesis was a part of the medical community's journey towards more truth.

Why All Beliefs Are *On the Way*

It's not just science that's like this. Beliefs about all topics, including meaning, relationships, and morality are no different from science in being *on the way*. Such beliefs don't have formal testing laboratories and peer review processes, but they, too, develop through this ongoing process of discovery, testing, communicating with others, and revision.

Being provisional doesn't make any of these beliefs invalid. It simply makes them partial—valuable guides that can become even more valuable as we broaden and deepen around them.

Consider beliefs about parenting. A new parent might believe that consistency is the most important factor in raising children. This belief likely comes from real observations and experiences—they've seen that children respond well to predictable routines and clear expectations. So this new parent acts on this belief about consistency: they establish bedtimes, create rules, and maintain boundaries.

But as they learn more—through trial and error, conversations with other parents, reading, observing their own children—their understanding becomes more nuanced. Maybe they discover that flexibility matters too, especially when a child is sick or stressed. Or that different children need different approaches: one thrives with structure while another needs more autonomy. Or that consistency in values matters more than consistency in rules.

Their original belief wasn't wrong—it captured something important about parenting. But their evolving understanding is richer and more useful. They've gained more truth about parenting, using the foundation of what they understood before.

This is how all our beliefs develop: through engagement with reality, feedback from experience, and dialogue with others who see differently. The process never ends because there's always more to learn.

The Freedom of Imperfect Knowledge

Recognizing that all our beliefs are "on the way" creates tremendous freedom:

Relief from the pressure to be right: You don't have to defend every detail of your worldview. You can acknowledge what you're still learning.

Curiosity instead of defensiveness: When someone challenges your beliefs, you can explore their perspective instead of automatically defending yours.

Growth without losing identity: You can update your views without feeling like you're betraying your core values or admitting you were foolish before.

Connection across difference: You can engage more meaningfully with people who see the world differently, treating them as sources of insight rather than threats to your certainty.

Practical Application: Holding Beliefs as Working Hypotheses

So how do you live this way practically? Think of your beliefs as working hypotheses—ideas that guide your actions while remaining open to refinement.

For example, you might believe that regular exercise is crucial for health. This belief shapes important decisions about how you spend your time and energy. But you can hold it as a working hypothesis: "Based on what I know now, exercise seems essential for wellbeing. I'll act on this belief while staying open to learning more about what kinds of exercise work best for me."

This approach allows you to:

- Act decisively based on your current understanding
- Stay alert to new information that might refine your approach
- Adjust your beliefs and behaviors as you learn
- Discuss your views with others without feeling threatened

When Someone Challenges Your Beliefs

Instead of seeing challenges as attacks, you can treat them as opportunities to test and refine your working hypotheses.

If someone disagrees with your views on education, politics, or relationships, you might respond with curiosity: "That's interesting. What experiences have shaped your perspective?" or "Help me understand how you see this differently."

This doesn't mean accepting every perspective as equally valid. Some ideas are better supported by evidence than others. But it does mean recognizing that even well-supported beliefs can benefit from examination and refinement.

Making Decisions Without Perfect Certainty

Living with provisional beliefs doesn't paralyze decision-making. Instead, it makes decisions more thoughtful and flexible:

- Gather the best available information while recognizing it may be incomplete.
- Act based on your current understanding while staying alert to signs you might need to adjust.
- Label your confidence levels: "I'm quite confident about this" vs. "This is my best guess with limited information."

- Treat decisions as experiments that provide feedback for future choices.
- Stay open to course corrections as new information emerges.

For instance, choosing a career path doesn't require perfect knowledge of your future interests or the job market. You can make the best decision you can with current information while remaining open to pivoting as you learn more about yourself and the world.

Daily Practices: Living with Provisional Beliefs

Before strong assertions

Pause and ask: "How confident am I about this? What might I be missing?" This simple check can transform declarations into explorations.

In conversations

Practice phrases that reflect provisional thinking:
- "From what I've seen..."
- "My current understanding is..."
- "I'm still learning about this, but..."
- "Help me understand how you see this..."

When feeling defensive

Notice defensiveness as a signal that a belief matters to you, then get curious: "What about this challenge feels threatening? What might I learn from this perspective?"

Reflect weekly

Choose one strong belief and explore it: What evidence supports it? What questions remain? How has your thinking evolved? What might you learn next?

The Ripple Effects of This Shift

When you begin treating truth as a journey rather than a possession, the effects extend far beyond individual beliefs:

- Relationships improve because you can engage difference with curiosity rather than hostility.
- Learning accelerates because you're genuinely open to new information and perspectives.
- Stress decreases because you're not constantly defending a perfect worldview.
- Wisdom grows because you can integrate insights from many sources without feeling like you're abandoning your values.
- Conversations deepen because people feel safe sharing their own evolving thoughts with you.

Recap & Reflection

Embracing truth as "on the way" doesn't weaken your mind or excuse intellectual laziness. In fact, I see it as rather the opposite: it's a call to stay sharp, to stay alert to what you might be missing, and to be eager—not just willing, but *eager*—to revise your views when you encounter new evidence and perspectives. Now *that* is intellectual fortitude!

You can learn to act on what you know while staying alert to what you don't. You can celebrate clarity without mistaking it for finality. You can treat uncertainty as a compass pointing toward growth rather than a threat to your stability.

This approach cultivates the intellectual virtues our world desperately needs: curiosity instead of dogmatism, humility instead of arrogance, patience instead of reactivity. These qualities allow genuine learning, meaningful dialogue, and sustainable growth to flourish.

When you see your beliefs as provisional hypotheses rather than permanent fixtures, conversations become opportunities to refine your understanding. Challenges become a chance to strengthen your thinking, and moments of doubt become doorways to deeper insight.

Living this way transforms truth from something you possess into something you participate in—a collaborative journey of discovery that connects you more deeply to reality and to other people seeking to understand it.

CHAPTER SEVEN

Improve Your Intellect by Healing Your Heart (Cultivating Inner Safety)

> In This Chapter, You Will...
> -Explore why cultivating inner safety—feeling secure in yourself and in the world—amplifies capacities for intellectual vulnerability
> -Examine how negative self-beliefs that make you feel unsafe in yourself can narrow curiosity, heighten defensiveness, and limit your capacity for growth
> -Examine how negative existential beliefs that make you resent the world can narrow curiosity, heighten defensiveness, and limit your capacity for growth
> -Develop greater awareness of how your emotions and attachments shape your thinking, giving you the tools to respond thoughtfully rather than reactively

A note before we begin: *This chapter explores connections between emotional wellbeing and intellectual openness. While I share approaches that have helped me and others, persistent negative beliefs that significantly impact daily life may benefit from professional support. If exploring these ideas brings up overwhelming emotions, consider working with a mental health professional you trust whose approach aligns with your values.*

Leaning Into, Not Away from, Emotions

Traditional approaches to intellectual development often treat emotions as obstacles to clear thinking. The assumption is that rational thought requires setting aside feelings and focusing purely on logic and evidence.

But this separation is an illusion. Our emotions and thoughts are deeply interconnected in a way that can never be overcome. When we feel threatened—whether physically, socially, or psychologically—our thinking naturally becomes more defensive and less exploratory. When we feel safe, we're more likely to remain curious and open to new information.

What if intellectual growth is not a matter of distance from emotions, but rather embracing them, leaning in—and becoming wiser in how to relate to them?

Fighting Certainty Addiction with Inner Safety

The central premise of this book is that we addict ourselves to certainty out of a drive for safety. We all long to feel at home in the world: solid, steady, and safe. We cling to our beliefs out of the illusion they will create this for us.

So while all the tools I share in this book help train our minds for intellectual vulnerability, the most powerful may be cultivating a foundation of inner safety.

Inner safety is the felt sense of "I am okay no matter what happens." It's a calm center in the middle of chaos—a steady peace that lives within you and doesn't depend too much on external circumstances.

We can all work toward creating this for ourselves.

Many factors contribute to inner safety that I won't address in this book: histories, traumas, systemic injustices, resource disparities, and physical health all play significant roles. These constitute complexities I'll leave for other contexts.

But I will put on your plate for consideration two specific paths to inner safety: examining negative beliefs you carry about yourself, and examining negative beliefs you carry about the world. When you do this, you may find that you wish to revise these negative beliefs into more neutral or positive ones, which can help you unlock more equanimity in yourself. You can create more inner safety you can rely on to stay centered, even when your most cherished beliefs feel threatened.

Curiosity about "I'm Not Okay as Myself" Beliefs

We don't usually think of our self-image as a set of beliefs, but that's exactly what it is.

- "I always mess things up,"
- "I'm broken,"
- "I'm no good,"
- "I don't deserve good things,"
- "I'm unacceptable as I am,"
- "I'm too sensitive, too aggressive, too..."

These are beliefs. They are not guaranteed truths. Any belief you carry about yourself may feel obviously true, but like all other beliefs, you learned them at some point in life from witnessing and experiencing whatever you witnessed and experienced.

And also like all other beliefs, they likely benefit from curious engagement, reflection, and revision.

Where do such beliefs come from? It's complicated, and experts differ on this, but it seems to me that we form negative self-beliefs out of our drive for safety: *if I'm hard on myself, I'll force myself to do what I must to belong and be safe.* Many critical moments of learning such things occur when we're very young—as early as infancy or early childhood. This can set the stage for everything that comes after. We can also go through significant traumas or live through difficult conditions as adults, setting the stage for everything else down the line.

We often learn such things either because we're directly told to, or it's implied. Sometimes, we figure out all our own that if we shame ourselves into behaving a certain way then we'll be more likely to be accepted by others. This results in negative self-beliefs, which is tragic, but it comes from our deeply-rooted drive to keep ourselves safe among other people. It's self-protection.

Yet as self-protective as negative self-beliefs can be, they can contribute to difficulty with all kinds of vulnerability, including with the intellect. Self-negativity can make us feel the need to:

- Perform a certain identity or role to belong
- Seem invulnerably smart to ourselves or others
- Cling tightly to ideas that offer stability in identity, belonging, or control

When we feel insufficient, we can become hypervigilant about how we are perceived, both by ourselves and others. We can also feel a deep woundedness that can drive us to seek out more external safety than we would otherwise. We can become "addicted to certainty," to compensate for that deep pain or wound.

Of course, self-negativity doesn't always lead to certainty addiction. But the pain and instability of it can make us more vulnerable to it.

Proactive Revision of Negative Self-Beliefs

Intellectual vulnerability invites curiosity about self-beliefs. If you have negative beliefs about yourself, why? Are they really true?

It also invites proactive reconsideration of these beliefs. You can get curious about and re-tell the story of who you are.

What stories of your being make the most sense to you?

"I'm okay as I am," "I'm as good as other people," "I try as hard as other people," "being wrong doesn't mean I'm stupid," and "I belong the same as anybody else," are some beliefs worth trying on for size. For everybody.

These can help us feel safer in our own beings, and therefore less beholden to external promises of safety.

When you begin shifting to a gentler relationship with yourself, you may experience more inner safety and less pressure to perform. Such change typically doesn't happen overnight, and can involve or may require various therapeutic modalities. But in general, you may find yourself less driven to cling to certainty (among myriad other sources of relief). You may relax that grip.

Once, it may have subconsciously felt like your survival hinged on contorting yourself to perform a specific identity, or fighting for your beliefs. But with gentle curiosity and acceptance of yourself, life can often become more of a gentle arena for exploring truth, even alongside people you once considered enemies.

An Example: My Father's Softer Side

My father is an excellent example of how inner, emotional safety can unlock intellectual growth.

About two years ago, I noticed a dramatic shift in his openness to new ideas. It was Thanksgiving. While everyone else busied themselves with chores, board games, or tending to their kids, Dad and I sat at the dining room table discussing political topics that once sparked major arguments.

He never raised his voice, talked over me, or insisted his view was the only logical one. Instead, he asked thoughtful questions and spoke softly. Then, at the end of the conversation, he said: "I may be wrong about this. You may be right."

I looked up at him in surprise. As better as our conversations has become in the preceding few years, he'd never said anything like that before. I began to laugh, and I ended up laughing so hard I fell out of my chair. From the floor and between chortles, I asked what inspired his newfound humility. "Dad. What's changed?"

"I'm developing my softer side!" he said, chuckling gently. "I'm a more sensitive guy than I used to be."

I laughed even harder, so hard my sides ached.

In the months that followed I pieced together that after retirement, my dad, who'd been raised by coal miners and steel plant workers who'd lived through the Depression in Detroit, had started getting more in touch with aspects of himself he'd repressed for the sake of being a tough guy. He relaxed into his being. He felt safer in who he was. This made him more open to listening and changing his mind.

"I love you so much, Dad," I gasped out, still laughing.

"I love you too, kid," he said.

Steps to Exploring and Rewriting "I'm Not Okay As Myself" Beliefs:

1. **Identify negative self-beliefs.**
2. **Reflect:** How were these beliefs learned? Were they protective at one time? Are they still serving you?
3. **Practice self-compassion:** Relax the impulse to shame or contort yourself to fit in.
4. **Ask:** Would I encourage someone else to think about themselves this way? If not, why do I do it to myself?
5. **Explore new beliefs gently:** "I belong as I am," "I'm okay no matter what happens," "I welcome change." Meditate on them intentionally. It often takes serious attention to change how you view and talk to yourself.
6. **Be patient with yourself.** Remember that changing long-held beliefs takes time, and progress isn't always linear.

Reminder: If you're struggling with persistent negative self-beliefs that significantly impact your daily life, or if exploring these beliefs brings up overwhelming emotions, consider finding a mental health professional you trust whose approach aligns with your values and can provide appropriate support. I also recommend content by psychotherapist Koorosh Rassekh.

The Danger of "The World Is Unacceptable as It Is" Beliefs

Existential beliefs about the nature of the universe matter for inner safety, too. Life is full of unpredictable events. We will all die. We are highly vulnerable here on Earth and will suffer. These are difficult things to make sense of. How we relate to these realities influences our capacity for intellectual openness.

Consider some existential beliefs that can degrade inner safety:

- "The universe is meaningless."
    - You may feel compelled to will your own meaning and purpose.
- "God is vengeful."
    - You may fear making mistakes.
- "I will face harsh judgment after death."
    - You may feel pressure to get things right.
- "Life is pure chaos."
    - You may shy away from risks.
- "There is no trustworthy higher power."
    - You may feel an increased need to personally control outcomes.

The relationship between existential beliefs and intellectual openness isn't straightforward. These beliefs don't automatically produce the specific responses I wrote here. For example, for some people, believing "life is meaningless" creates a need to impose their own values and meaning on life, but it can liberate others from the pressure to be right. Similarly, believing "life is chaotic" can create anxiety that fuels certainty addiction, or it can spark curiosity and adaptability. The key question is: Do your existential beliefs help you feel at home in the world, or do they keep you in a state of resistance and fear?

You'll also note that some of these examples include God and some do not. Inner safety isn't predicated on being a believer of any sort. I'm not encouraging any particular flavor of belief or disbelief. I'm encouraging existential exploration for homecoming, trust, and acceptance, whatever that looks like for you.

It can help to look back to how you learned your existential beliefs. For example, I grew up without spirituality, resulting in feelings of isolation and resentment about a universe without God. This gave me a deep drive to will my own meaning, to derive satisfaction from identity and success, and to control outcomes. All these things degraded my inner safety. It's taken me many years to untangle this and arrive at relative existential peace, but I've done it. I look forward to doing more.

My friend Robert (whose men's group we met in chapter five) has been on a very different existential journey. He was raised in a traditional religious community in the rural mid-West in the 1950s. He recently dove deep into his past and figured out that when he was a child he learned that he needed to be fully correct about what was real and good or else he'd face eternal judgment from God. He also figured out that this was driving some difficult feelings of unsafety with his friend who was exploring new political beliefs and allegiances. Robert began working on softening this high expectation for being correct. He now finds himself more at home with intellectual vulnerability, feeling more ease with his newly conservative friend and others, and is helping some other friends do the same.

The Goal: Not Perfect Safety, But Trust and Acceptance

The reality of human existence is that it is unsafe. Uncertainty, loss, suffering, and eventual death are in the cards for all of us. The goal of existential exploration isn't to eliminate all uncertainty or guarantee perfect safety. You won't achieve that. The goal is to develop greater acceptance—trust, belonging, and okayness within the realities of existence.

The path to existential peace looks different for everyone. Whether through religion, spirituality, or philosophy, you can explore ways to release control of outcomes and feel more at home in the world. These explorations can help you develop trust that you'll be okay, including during difficult conversations, personal changes, or periods of confusion and uncertainty.

Steps to Examining "The World Isn't Okay" Beliefs:

1. **Identify** your current beliefs about life, existence, and meaning.
2. **Ask**: How did I come to hold these beliefs? Are they necessarily true?
3. **Explore concepts** of trust and acceptance.
4. **Investigate alternatives**: books, conversations, spiritual communities, spiritual practices, and philosophical frameworks are all great options.
5. **Consider approaches** that help you feel safer amidst uncertainty.
6. **Engage new perspectives** within or outside your present community to expand your understanding.

- **Tip**: *The overall goal for inner safety:* "I'm okay; I will be okay; I can accept what is and what comes; I don't need to defend my beliefs at all costs."

-

Cultivating Awareness

Even as you cultivate inner safety, you will always (along with the rest of us) be influenced by your experiences, attachments, and beliefs. This is part of being human.

So to round out the cultivation of inner safety for intellectual vulnerability, you can cultivate awareness. You can notice the things that make you feel unsafe and how you tend to respond. You can learn about your own attachments and strong reactions.

Then, in any moment of thinking or talking with others, you can use that awareness to help you choose your response.

For example, I tend to feel defensive when people imply that science and faith are enemies. I've spent many years exploring different definitions of faith and how faith doesn't have to oppose science. It's emotionally important to me, so the notion that they're enemies activates my defenses. Knowing this helps me pause and talk myself down when I begin to activate.

I also dislike when people talk badly about their political opponents. I begin to activate and sometimes feel tempted to cut them out of my life. We have different core values, after all! But I'm aware that this is a bias driven by my own vision for the world. I never want to cease learning from people who offer valuable pushback to my positions, so I take a deep breath and welcome them in.

Awareness is noticing how our beliefs, emotions, and attachments influence our thinking, then using it to help us choose.

Exercises for Awareness

Map your beliefs: Write down what you hold strongly and why. Rate your level of certainty and emotional attachment.

Tell your story: Reflect on how early life experiences may have shaped your current beliefs.

Identify triggers: Notice which topics provoke strong reactions and explore why.

Observe identity, belonging, and control: See how these psychological levers influence what you defend and how you argue.

Keep a curiosity journal: Record moments of strong judgment or conviction, explore their roots, and look for patterns over time.

The Broader Vision

When we understand how emotional wellbeing supports intellectual growth, we begin to see that taking care of our psychological health (including everything beyond the scope of this chapter) isn't separate from developing our minds—it's an essential part of it.

This doesn't mean you need to resolve all emotional patterns before engaging intellectually with the world. Rather, it means that awareness of these patterns can help you think more clearly and engage more generously with others.

As you develop this intention and awareness, you're not just becoming a better thinker—you're becoming someone who can hold complexity, sit with uncertainty, and remain curious about perspectives that challenge your own. These qualities serve you well in every area of life.

Recap & Reflection

Can you dislodge some barriers to vulnerability with gentle curiosity about your beliefs? By gently examining negative self-beliefs and challenging existential assumptions, you may improve your feelings of inner safety and therefore can create more space for dialogue, insight, and surprise.

Awareness can amplify this process, giving you the ability to notice triggers, reflect, and respond with intention rather than react automatically.

Cultivating inner safety isn't simple, and so much more can be discussed and implemented than what's in this chapter. But I hope to stimulate your curiosity about what you believe about yourself and the world, leading to at least a little bit more.

As with all things, with inner safety I invite you to be *on the way*.

CHAPTER EIGHT

If You Want to Persuade, Stop Trying to Persuade

> In This Chapter, You Will...
>
> -Learn to recognize the subtle ways persuasion can create resistance, and why curiosity, respect, and genuine participation are more effective tools for influence
>
> -Find practical exercises to shift from a mindset of persuasion to one of participation, allowing you to engage others productively while deepening your own understanding
>
> -Explore releasing control of outcomes and decentering yourself from truth

You're Racist!

A family member was once furious about surveillance cameras being installed in a neighborhood where most of the foot traffic was Black. Local politicians were suggesting that the employees monitoring the CCTV should also be Black. To him, it seemed obvious: the reason was so Black people could "let Black people off the hook."

I had a choice for how to respond. I could have flown off the handle, saying something like, "You're racist!" Instead, I listened, then said: "Okay, I get why you might infer that based on what this newscaster is saying and your context and experience. Can I share something I've read recently that I find interesting?"

"Of course," he said. Then, I told him about a scientific paper I'd just read showing how people are generally better at recognizing faces resembling their own racial group, presumably from repeated exposure. I also expressed that I'd personally experienced this. I'd lived in China and noticed that over the course of my time there I got better at seeing nuance in Chinese bone structure I hadn't seen before.

He said, "Wow, I didn't know that. Maybe these politicians want to change the race of the surveillance employees to make it more fair, not less."

I said, "Seems like it to me!" I didn't have to take him to that conclusion at all. I simply offered from my perspective as if I, too, were on the way learning about all these things (which I was, and remain).

Now, what would have happened if I had leaped down his throat and called him out for being racist?

What kind of learning and growth do we unlock when we stop trying to shame and castigate people into agreeing with us?

The Psychology Behind Persuasion's Failure

Direct persuasion attempts often backfire. Why? When people perceive that someone is trying to control their beliefs, they experience what psychologists call "reactance"—a motivational drive to restore their threatened freedom by holding even more tightly to their original position.

This defensive response is compounded by our tendency to protect existing beliefs and identity when we reason. We're very skilled at generating counterarguments and finding flaws in perspectives that threaten our own.

Since most of us associate our beliefs with our identities, when we try to change someone's beliefs, we often unintentionally make them feel like we are trying to change *them*. Persuasion also implies, if unintentionally, that you think they're wrong, which is a source of embarrassment and shame.

While you may have something very important to share, the more you try to force this person to change their beliefs, the more threatened they will feel. This makes you far less likely to affect change and far more likely to alienate them and create close-mindedness and animosity.

Conversely, when people feel their autonomy is respected, they're more likely to genuinely consider the substance of ideas rather than reflexively defending against them. When you stop trying to control someone's beliefs and instead engage them as a capable thinking partner, you're more likely to influence their thinking—because you're working *with* rather than *against* their psychological makeup.

Trade Persuasion for Participation

I suggest a shift from persuasion to what I call "participation."

Participation means:
- Contributing your perspective curiously, humbly, and openly
- Asking questions and offering ideas you think might enrich people's thinking, without being forceful
- Approaching others as if they have insight that can broaden and deepen your understanding of reality, which they do
- Learning from them, as you hope they'll learn from you

Participation isn't about abandoning your values or avoiding difficult topics. It's about participating. You act as one of eight billion seekers of truth. You share your little bit while learning from others sharing theirs. You show them your map of reality while you take a gander at theirs.

Traditional persuasion asks: "How can I make this person think like me?"

Participation asks: "How can I ask questions or offer insight that helps this person move toward truth, whether that means agreeing with me or not? And how can I learn from them at the same time?"

This shift transforms the entire dynamic. Instead of opponents in a battle for truth, you become collaborators in an exploration. Instead of defending views from specific mountaintops, you're revising your maps together.

When you participate rather than push, you invite dialogue, model curiosity, and create space for organic influence. Sharing ideas while honoring others' perspectives facilitates intellectual growth more effectively than force ever could.

Participation doesn't mean you must abandon your convictions (though it does invite being open to revision at least). It means offering ideas without controlling the outcome—contributing, instead of controlling.

Seek Mutual Enrichment

A great goal for any conversation is mutual enrichment. You can enrich others by sharing from your perspective, and they can enrich you if you're open to listening to theirs.

You don't have to agree with a person about anything, and you can still learn from them. In fact, it's often from the people most different from us that we learn the most.

People can even be dead wrong about things, and you can learn from them. You can deepen your understanding of what it's like to be them and people like them. This can enhance your ability to reason with them as well as find solutions across your differences down the line.

Approaching each conversation as a learning opportunity is the most effective way to transform the dynamic from war to partnership. It signals to your conversation partner that you value their perspective and are genuinely curious, not seeking to dominate or "win." This creates a shared exploration rather than a contest, which makes people more open, reflective, and willing to engage.

Every exchange becomes a chance to expand your own thinking while fostering connection and mutual respect.

Release Control and Decenter Yourself

Most of us hold ourselves at the center of truth. We think that we need to make other people think like us for the world to become a safer and more just place.

But the honest reality is that none of us are guaranteed to be closer to the truth than others (I heartily include myself in this).

So for the sake of truth, we can—and I believe should—decenter ourselves. We can offer our ideas, then let our conversation partners chew on what we've shared. We can let them walk their own paths to truth—whether that means agreeing with us or not.

Ultimately, this is all we can do anyway, because belief change happens gradually and at its own pace. It cannot be forced. Ideas need to germinate before they can sprout. People need to work through their own thoughts in their own time.

So releasing control of outcomes is both the most honorable and the most effective thing you can do.

It's possible any person you chat with will not end up agreeing with you, and that's okay. Maybe it's for the best, ultimately. You can't know for sure you're the correct one. All you can do is your own personal best participating, contributing, and learning.

Practical Strategies for Participation

Before the conversation: Check your intentions

Notice what you're hoping to achieve. Are you genuinely curious about their perspective, or are you looking for openings to prove them wrong?

Instead of: "I need to show them why they're mistaken about climate change."

Try: "I wonder what I can share that will enrich their thinking, and what experiences have shaped their views on environmental issues."

During the conversation: create space for exploration

Use language that opens rather than closes dialogue. Try:

- "I've been thinking about this differently, and I'm curious how you see it..."
- "That's an interesting point. Help me understand how you arrived at that conclusion..."
- "I've had different experiences with this issue. Would you be interested in hearing about them?"

My personal favorite is to use language of wonder: "I wonder about the bigger implications..."

I also like to share what I'm thinking about my blind spots or biases, which can stimulate others to reflect on their own: "I feel some heightened emotions and like I might be reasoning to protect my identity right now. Maybe we can explore that together, or I can explore it later and let you know the outcome next time we chat."

Share your perspective as one voice, not the final word

When offering your views, frame them as contributions to ongoing exploration rather than definitive conclusions:

Instead of: "Studies prove that you're wrong about this."

Try: "I've been reading some research that suggests a different possibility. What do you make of this?"

Ask questions that illuminate rather than trap

Good questions help both of you understand their reasoning. Try:
- "What experiences have shaped your thinking on this?"
- "What would it look like if your approach were implemented?"
- "What concerns do you have about the alternative I've suggested?"

Exercises for Developing Participation Skills

The Curiosity Reset

Before entering potentially difficult conversations, spend two minutes writing answers (in your notes app, or etc) to these questions:
- What do I genuinely want to learn from this person?
- What assumptions might I be making about their position?
- How can I contribute something valuable without trying to control the outcome?

The Steel Man Practice

To "straw man" an argument is to engage the weakest version of it: you make it into a *straw man* so you can easily knock it down. Steel manning is the opposite. Choose someone whose views you find problematic. Write a small paragraph summarizing their position that they would recognize as fair and accurate. Try to defend their position as well as they do or even better. Understand the values that drive it. This exercise helps you understand their actual reasoning rather than a caricature of it.

The Perspective Inventory

After conversations where you felt defensive or frustrated, reflect:

- What was I trying to protect or prove?
- What might the other person have been trying to protect or prove?
- What did I learn about their values, even if I disagree with their conclusions?
- How might I approach a similar conversation differently?

Double Up Questions

In your next three conversations about topics you care deeply about, challenge yourself to ask twice as many questions as you make statements. Notice how this changes the dynamic and what you learn.

The Learning Index

After a conversation where you listened, index what you learned. If you can't think of anything, dig deeper. You may not have encountered any information that prompted you to change your mind in a significant way, but you still learned about what it's like to be this other person and others who share similar views. Another thing you'll have learned is about how to engage and work with this mindset in the future, a crucial skill for problem solving in diverse groups or society at large.

Measuring Success Differently

When you shift from persuasion to participation, you also need to change how you measure success. Instead of asking "Did I convince them?" ask:

- Did we both learn something new?
- Do we understand each other's positions more clearly?
- Did I contribute something valuable to their thinking?
- Did the conversation strengthen or damage our relationship?
- Am I more curious about their perspective than I was before?
- Did I model the kind of engagement I hope to see in the world?

These questions reflect a different vision of productive dialogue—one focused on mutual enrichment rather than ideological victory.

The Ripple Effects

When you consistently approach disagreement with curiosity rather than control, several things happen:

- People become more open with you because they trust that you won't attack them for sharing their honest thoughts.
- Your own thinking improves because you're genuinely engaging with the strongest versions of opposing views rather than dismissing them.
- You model constructive dialogue for others, potentially influencing how they approach their own difficult conversations.
- Relationships deepen even across significant disagreement because people feel respected and heard.
- You become more persuasive precisely because you've stopped trying to persuade—people are more influenced by those who respect their autonomy and intelligence.

Recap & Reflection

The paradox of persuasion—that trying to control others' beliefs often strengthens their resistance—points toward a more effective and ethical approach to influence: participation.

When you engage with genuine curiosity, respect others' autonomy, and contribute to shared understanding rather than trying to control outcomes, you create conditions where real learning and growth become possible.

This doesn't mean abandoning your values. It simply means being respectful and curious about what others might teach you. Stay kind and open and see what happens.

In a world full of people trying to convince each other through force and manipulation, choosing to participate rather than persuade is both a radical act and a return to the collaborative spirit that makes genuine dialogue possible.

CHAPTER NINE

Strengthening Scholarship & Society with Uncertainty

> In This Chapter, You Will...
> -Learn to recognize and move beyond fear-driven pressures in academia
> -Engage opposing views at their best
> -Create higher quality discourse in academia and beyond
> -Foster renewed trust in scholarship and scholarly institutions
> -See how admitting uncertainty, embracing dialogue, and questioning assumptions can improve the quality of intellectual arguments we produce in and outside of academia

Rigorous Argument Building for Academia and Beyond

Scholarship aspires to pursue truth through rigorous inquiry, yet academic culture often rewards certainty over discovery. If we transform how we research, dialogue, and educate, we can create powerful ripple effects in higher education and beyond.

This chapter is about crafting quality intellectual arguments, but as this art concerns sources, dialogue partners, and how we relate to both things, improvements in this domain translate to widespread improvements across culture—including more dynamic dialogue, more fluid exchange across divides, enhanced public discourse and trust, and communal truth seeking. The chapter is written with scholars and students in mind, but it's for anybody interested in the immediate and long-term benefits of vulnerable inquiry.

The Paradox of Academic Certainty

Academic culture presents scholars with a curious paradox: have good ideas, but then spend your career defending them, not revising. We know that insight evolves—Aristotle stimulated and gave way to Aquinas, then Bacon, then Hume, and on and on—yet we often write and speak as if our current understanding represents the final word.

This tension creates what we might call "performative certainty": the professional habit of presenting arguments with more confidence than evidence warrants, or entrenching yourself in a view or methodology because you've already staked a claim in it. While understandable given the competitive nature of academic careers, this tendency may undermine the very goals of scholarly inquiry.

What if intellectual vulnerability enhances rather than threatens scholarly excellence?

The Hidden Costs of Defensive Scholarship

Most academics recognize several pressures that shape scholarly behavior:

- **Publish or perish:** You must publish a high quantity of papers.
- **Secure grants:** You must find your own funding.
- **Build reputation:** You must create an identity that people consider authoritative.
- **Defend turf:** You must fight for the superiority of your methods and ideas.

These pressures, while real, can lead to defensive practices that compromise intellectual integrity:

Tribalism over truth-seeking: *aligning with fashionable theories or established schools of thought to secure professional belonging, even when evidence suggests more complex realities.* For example: a sociologist might dismiss quantitative methods not because they're inappropriate for the research question, but because their department values qualitative approaches.

Straw-manning opponents: *presenting rival perspectives in their weakest form to make our own arguments appear stronger, rather than engaging with the most sophisticated versions of competing ideas.* For example: a philosopher might critique a caricatured version of utilitarianism rather than engaging with its most careful formulations.

Premature closure: *moving too quickly from hypothesis to conclusion, avoiding the messiness of genuine inquiry that might complicate preferred narratives.* For example, a scholar might consider research done once they've read enough to support their arguments.

Jargon as armor: *using specialized terminology not to achieve precision, but to signal membership in particular academic communities and deflect scrutiny from outsiders.* For example: a scholar might dismiss a colleague's thoughtful critique because they used contrarian or seemingly outdated terminology, rather than engaging with the substance of their argument.

These habits aren't born of malice—they're survival strategies in an often punishing professional environment. But they extract a cost: they distance us from the very curiosity and openness that make discovery and mutual enrichment possible.

Intellectual Vulnerability as Scholarly Strength

Consider what changes when we approach our work—and one another—with intellectual vulnerability:

Enhanced Rigor Through Uncertainty

When you acknowledge what you don't know (which often means admitting what you haven't read, or what theories or approaches you're less familiar with), you force yourself to be more precise about what you do know.

Intellectual vulnerability is a tool for identifying exactly where your argument stands on solid ground, where it doesn't venture, and where it may venture into speculation. This precision strengthens rather than weakens your scholarly contributions, and helps you communicate more authentically at the edges of your expertise. This invites others to do the same.

Deeper Engagement with Opposing Views

Instead of seeking the weakest version of competing perspectives, intellectual vulnerability invites engagement with their strongest formulations. This doesn't mean molding your arguments to be inclusive of every scholar or thought you encounter. But it does mean taking seriously the possibility that your opponents have more nuance than it seems or might see something you've missed.

Can you learn from opponents? Can you create more nuance in your own theory or argument because of what they say? This will not weaken but strengthen your work.

Dynamic Rather Than Static Arguments

Instead of defending fixed positions, you can present your work as contributing to ongoing conversations. This allows your arguments to evolve as you encounter new evidence and perspectives, making your scholarship more responsive to genuine discovery.

More Open and Plural Conversations

Honoring others as equally well-intended truth-seekers helps all of us, perhaps especially in academic settings and institutions, speak more freely and safely. It enables us to seek truth less encumbered by personal defense and more equipped to devise new theories and find new solutions.

The Practice of Steel-Manning Your Opponents

One of the most transformative applications of intellectual vulnerability in scholarship is learning to quote and engage opponents at their strongest rather than their weakest. "Steel-Manning" (explained in chapter eight), requires more effort but produces several benefits:

Stronger arguments: When you engage the best version of opposing views, you're forced to develop more sophisticated responses. Your critique becomes more meaningful because it addresses actual rather than caricatured positions.

Expanded understanding: Seriously engaging with intelligent opponents often reveals complexities you hadn't considered. Even when you ultimately disagree, you develop a more nuanced understanding of the issue at stake.

Professional credibility: Colleagues recognize fair, nuanced engagement when they see it. Scholars who consistently misrepresent opponents eventually lose credibility, while those known for fair representation earn respect across disciplinary boundaries.

Give your opponents, especially those still living with whom you may be able to talk later, the benefit of the doubt. Don't make straw men of them for the sake of strengthening your own argument or image of intellectual superiority. It may likely weaken you in the long run. Quote them at their best.

A Personal Example of Finding Significant Consonance Across Divides

During my doctoral work, I became fascinated by the nature-nurture debate—the question of whether genetics or culture plays a larger role in human development and behavior. This debate has generated enormous literature and considerable acrimony between different camps.

As I read deeply in both biological and cultural approaches, I noticed something troubling: scholars on both sides seemed to be arguing against caricatures rather than engaging with the most sophisticated versions of opposing views. Biologically-oriented researchers were characterized as genetic determinists who ignored environmental factors, while culturally-oriented scholars were portrayed as naive blank-slate theorists who denied biological realities.

But when I read the primary sources carefully, I found that the most serious thinkers on both sides acknowledged the importance of both nature and nurture. The real disagreements were more subtle—about mechanisms, timing, and relative influence in specific contexts. The apparent warfare between camps seemed largely based on misrepresentation and selective quotation.

This experience taught me that some of our most heated academic debates, including those with major cultural implications—nature versus nurture, humanities versus the sciences, religion versus science—are less fundamental than they appear. We agree on a lot more than we think.

When we engage opponents at their best rather than their worst, we often discover more common ground than we expected. The remaining disagreements become more focused and productive.

Practical Applications for Scholars and Students

Before writing: The Assumption Audit

Before drafting your next paper or chapter, list three core assumptions underlying your argument. For each assumption, ask: What would change about my analysis if this assumption were false or incomplete? This exercise often reveals unstated premises that deserve explicit attention.

While reading: Charitable Interpretation

We all instinctively react to ideas based on their degree of alignment with our present thinking, then give the purveyor more or less benefit of the doubt. This predisposes us to interpret subsequent statements with relatively more charity or suspicion.

While reading, monitor your reactions. Notice whether you're feeling charitable or suspicious toward the author. Explore why, and decide with intention how to proceed. Try to keep yourself in a place where you can read with a neutral or charitable lens. You can still assess critically in the end; the point is to deliberate with the clearest mind possible.

During research: The Steel-Man Reading

When encountering sources that disagree with your position, try to understand why intelligent, well-informed people might hold these views. What evidence or experiences might lead them to their conclusions? This doesn't require agreement, but it does require taking seriously the possibility that they might see something you've missed.

You can strengthen essays if you devote paragraphs or whole sections to exploring this.

While writing: Qualify Claims Appropriately

Academic writing often defaults to stronger claims than evidence warrants. Practice distinguishing between what your research strongly supports, what it suggests tentatively, and what remains genuinely uncertain. This precision makes your actual claims more credible.

While peer reviewing: Constructive Uncertainty

When reviewing another's work, consider leading with questions rather than corrections: "Have you considered how X might complicate this argument?" or "What would it mean for your thesis if Y were true?" This approach can be more generative than simple rejection or criticism.

It's also possible that this person's argument doesn't need to consider X or mention Y. Look inwards at yourself and examine your own biases and desires here. We all conduct review using our own knowledge and perspective. Not all arguments need to include them.

In cross-disciplinary dialogue: Intentional Enrichment

Academic departments and journals can function as echo chambers, limiting exposure to perspectives that might challenge or enrich thinking. Intellectual vulnerability invites actively seeking out such perspectives. Consider attending talks or reading journals outside your immediate field. Wonder: *what could this other approach contribute to my understanding and research?* The goal isn't to become an expert in every field, but to remain curious about how different approaches might illuminate your own questions. This can have the added benefit of giving you a unique skillset and niche.

In all engagement: Language Awareness

New terminology often emerges from genuine attempts at precision, but language norms can evolve rapidly in academic communities, sometimes creating barriers between well-intentioned scholars. In many circles, language quickly becomes either "right" or "wrong" to use, prohibiting exchange with potentially high-quality interlocutors.

When writing, ask yourself: Am I using this term because it's necessary for clarity, or because it signals belonging to a particular community? When reading others' work, practice generous interpretation across evolving language conventions—the substance of an argument may be strong even when terminology differs from current norms. There's no such thing as perfectly precise language; it behooves us all to release rigidity and speak and interpret as generously as possible.

Teaching with Intellectual Vulnerability

For those involved in education, intellectual vulnerability transforms pedagogy as well as research:

- **Acknowledge what you don't know:** When students ask questions you can't answer, treat this as an opportunity for collective inquiry rather than professional embarrassment.
- **Think out loud:** Show students your reasoning process, including moments of uncertainty or revision.
- **Encourage productive disagreement:** Create classroom environments where students feel safe challenging ideas—including your own.
- **Assign your critics:** Include readings that challenge your own perspective in your syllabi.

Exercises for Scholarly Practice

Uncertainty Mapping

For your current research project, create three categories: (1) Claims strongly supported by evidence, (2) Plausible hypotheses requiring further investigation, (3) Genuinely open questions.

Notice how this affects the confidence with which you present different aspects of your work.

Cross-Disciplinary Exploration

Identify a question central to your research and spend time exploring how scholars in a different field approach similar questions. What methods, assumptions, or insights might transfer to your own work?

Vulnerable Presenting

In your next conference presentation or seminar, include a slide about limits of your theory, what you're still uncertain about, or what questions your research has generated. Notice how audiences respond to this honesty.

The Ripple Effects of Vulnerable Scholarship

When scholars practice intellectual vulnerability, the effects extend beyond individual careers:

Enhanced public trust: At a time when academic expertise faces skepticism, scholars who acknowledge uncertainty and engage opponents fairly may help rebuild public confidence in scholarly institutions.

Improved policy recommendations: Research that honestly acknowledges its limitations and engages with competing perspectives provides policymakers with more realistic assessments of what we know and don't know.

Cross-cutting collaboration: Many of society's most pressing challenges—climate change, inequality, technological disruption, culture wars—require insights from multiple disciplines. Scholars practiced in intellectual vulnerability may be better equipped for such collaboration.

Training future thinkers: Students who learn to think with intellectual vulnerability may be better prepared for careers requiring adaptability, critical thinking, and constructive engagement with difference.

Recap & Reflection

Intellectual vulnerability reframes scholarship as pilgrimage rather than conquest—a journey toward understanding rather than possession of final answers. And it happens better when we read our opponents charitably, as opposed to suspiciously. This doesn't weaken intellectual output; it strengthens it by keeping us responsive to evidence, open to revision, responsible to others walking similar paths, and committed to genuine discovery.

When we approach our work this way, we contribute not just to the accumulation of knowledge but to the cultivation of intellectual virtues our society desperately needs: curiosity over dogmatism, humility over arrogance, dialogue over debate. In an era of unprecedented challenges, embracing uncertainty across culture, including in the scholarly institutions that are the cornerstone of public discourse, may end up our greatest strength.

CHAPTER TEN

Beyond Politics: How Intellectual Vulnerability Transforms Health, Inner Peace, and Spirit

In This Chapter, You Will...
-Explore how intellectual vulnerability may help transform your physical health, inner dialogue, and spiritual peace
-Learn to approach personal challenges with curiosity instead of rigid assumptions
-Discover how questioning your beliefs about health, yourself, and the meaning of life can unlock new possibilities

Beyond Political Conversations

So far, we've focused primarily on how intellectual vulnerability can improve our relationships, political dialogue, and social connections. But the benefits extend far beyond our interactions with others.

The same curiosity that helps you listen to opposing viewpoints can revolutionize how you approach your health, your relationship with yourself, and your deepest questions about life's meaning. When you apply the principles of intellectual vulnerability to these personal domains, you open doors to growth that might otherwise remain locked.

The key insight is this: just as you hold beliefs about politics and society that benefit from examination, you also hold beliefs about your body, your worth, your capabilities, and your meaning that benefit from examination.

The content in this chapter is highly simplified, truncated, and architected from my own learnings and experiences. It also happens to touch on very important topics: health, self-perception, and spirituality. These are complex domains where trusted professionals can be invaluable. What follows reflects my personal experience and shouldn't replace professional support in areas you feel you need it.

The Common Thread: Question Limiting Assumptions

Before diving into specific areas, let's identify the common pattern. In each domain of life, we operate based on assumptions that feel obviously true but may actually be constraining us:

About physical health: "This is just how my body works," or "My doctor knows everything," or "Nothing will help my condition."

About our relationships with ourselves: "I'm not the kind of person who..." or "I always fail at..." or "I'm not good enough for..."

About the universe and meaning of life: "I've figured out what life is about," or "Those other spiritual perspectives are wrong," or "There's no point in entertaining my doubts and questions about what I believe."

These assumptions aren't necessarily wrong, but they become problems when we never examine them. Intellectual vulnerability invites us to wonder: What if some of these beliefs are outdated, incomplete, or unnecessarily limiting? What becomes possible when we approach them with curiosity—as if we're on the way broadening and deepening our understanding of reality, including ourselves?

Physical Health: Your Body as a Fascinating System of Cause and Effect

When it comes to physical health, intellectual vulnerability invites treating your body as a complex system worthy of curiosity. What's happening in your body giving rise to your experience? Why? Can something be done about it?

It's an oversimplification, but generally speaking, inputs (food, water, sleep, exercise, sunlight, stress, relationships, beliefs, etc) plus genetics give rise to outputs (energy, feeling, pain, health). How might you change inputs to improve outputs?

Diagnoses are often treated as inevitabilities, and symptoms are often discussed as if they cannot be helped. But many conditions that are presented as fixed realities may have more room for improvement than we're initially told. Digestive issues, autoimmunity, chronic fatigue, chronic pain, and other conditions: they can't always be healed or even improved, but sometimes they can be managed better if we stay curious about our bodies and how to best support them.

This doesn't mean dismissing medical expertise. It means recognizing that medicine is an evolving science with significant gaps and unknowns, and each person only knows as much as they personally know. Sometimes staying curious about your own experience can lead to insights that help you.

A Personal Example: Overcoming Chronic Pain I was Told I'd Have Forever

Until about a year ago, I dealt with chronic, near daily headaches since adolescence. I've spent countless nights sitting on the cold tiles of various bathroom floors with my head on the toilet seat breathing deeply and staying incredibly still. For two decades, I accepted the explanation I'd been given: some people are just unlucky with headaches.

But when my condition worsened significantly in my mid-thirties, I decided to approach it with intellectual vulnerability. Instead of accepting "this is just how I am," I resolved to dislodge my assumptions about the nature of pain and exercise curiosity until I found a more satisfying answer.

Which I ultimately did, resulting in a major reduction in pain.

I didn't have a health professional I could work with at the time. If I could have worked with one, I would have. But I didn't, so I set off reading and getting data about my health on my own. I read hundreds of articles on the nervous system, digestive system, muscular-skeletal system, eye health, pain, inflammation, and the like. I got bloodwork and X-rays done. Because I wasn't working with a life-threatening condition, I also conducted experiments on myself I knew were safe (but which I also knew might have negative effects) like trying a supplement or diet strategy to see what happened.

Today, I believe that structural issues in my skeleton, muscles, and nerves from an injury I endured as an infant are the core underlying cause of my pain. Since I pieced together this theory, I have been doing extensive chiropractic and physical therapy work, and it has dramatically improved my quality of life. Most days, today, I am pain free.

Many people watched me on this journey and expressed skepticism. *Shouldn't you just accept what you've been told?* But I persisted in questioning my and other people's assumptions to create better theories until I found one that seems to have enough truth to work.

Today, I am continuing to study pain, with the goal of becoming even more pain-free. I feel relatively confident that as I keep updating my understanding of pain, I'll keep finding new ways to combat or ultimately relieve it. I have no way to know that for sure, but I can stay curious, keep learning, and be gentle with myself and my body as I explore possibilities.

Health journeys don't always end up like this. We don't always solve pain, symptoms, or conditions. We don't even always reduce them. But we don't know what's possible until we begin exploring it.

Curiosity, it seems to me, may be the most underappreciated asset we have for improving our health.

(Note: The approach I took worked for my chronic headaches—a debilitating but not immediately life-threatening condition. For acute or potentially serious symptoms, professional evaluation is essential.)

We Know Less Than We Think, and That's Okay

Our culture's knowledge about diet, nutrition, and health has grown enormously, but it's still riddled with mistakes and gaps. Think about the changing views on eggs: decades ago, egg yolks were shunned for their cholesterol content. Today, we understand the body produces cholesterol on its own, and eggs—especially yolks—are nutrient powerhouses that can be a healthy component of most diets.

Fat and carbs have both swung from villain to hero and back again.

Or think about gut health. Fifteen years ago, "intestinal permeability" sounded like quackery to most. Today, it's an active area of research valued by many.

This is the nature of science: provisional and evolving. That's okay. We absolutely should use it. The trick is simply to stay as informed as possible, study broadly, make the best decisions we can, work with professionals we trust, and keep adjusting as new information comes out.

What will we know tomorrow? What are we doing today that we'll look back on tomorrow and think was backwards, maybe even barbaric? I expect a lot more than we imagine. I look forward to finding out.

Practical Application: Be Your Own Health Advocate

You can apply intellectual vulnerability to your health by:

Getting curious about patterns: Notice what makes you feel energetic versus drained, what foods leave you satisfied versus hungry an hour later, what activities boost versus sap your mood.

Questioning health assumptions: "I'm not a morning person"—what if that's changeable? "I need coffee to function"—what if there are other energy sources worth exploring?

Experimenting safely: Try one change at a time, track how you feel, and work with healthcare providers you trust when making significant adjustments.

Staying humble about what we and you don't know: Health science is constantly evolving. What seems certain today may be refined tomorrow.

Recognizing when DIY exploration is and isn't appropriate: There's a difference between exploring dietary changes for chronic fatigue and self-treating chest pain. Use good judgment about when curiosity is helpful versus when immediate professional care is necessary.

Inner Peace: How Self-Beliefs Influence Feelings & Possibilities

As a practice that concerns all beliefs, as explained briefly in chapter seven, intellectual vulnerability also invites curiosity about **self-beliefs**: the often subconscious stories we tell about who we are, what we deserve, and what we're capable of.

What might you unlock for yourself with gentle curiosity about what it means to be you?

Self-Beliefs Are Beliefs Like Any Other

We don't usually think of our self-image as a set of beliefs. But that's exactly what it is. "I'm not good at public speaking," "I'm too sensitive," "I always mess things up," "I'm not creative," "I'm not acceptable as I am," "I'm no good": these are beliefs. They are not facts, even when they feel obviously true.

And just like all other beliefs, they likely benefit from curious engagement, reflection, and revision.

One key question you can ask about your negative self-beliefs is: why?

If you have negative beliefs about yourself, why? Where did they come from?

I invite your curiosity. How and why do humans form negative self-beliefs? There are many theories about this. One perspective I find compelling (which I shared a bit of in chapter seven) suggests that negative self-beliefs slot into place out of survival value. The subconscious logic here is that if you are hard on yourself first, you will force yourself to behave as you think you should, thereby sparing yourself from shame or rejection by others. You will survive if you shame yourself into doing what you must.

This can begin as early as infancy, when acceptance is a literal matter of life or death. As an infant, if you don't secure the care of the adults around you, you will not be fed, and you will die. So infants have very powerful learning machinery in place. They learn to behave however they must to get the care they need to survive.

Young kids are much the same. They are vulnerable beings who need the adults in their lives to feed them, clothe them, and take them to school and such things. They learn to believe and do what they deem they must. If they're explicitly told or it's implied *you're not sufficient as you are*—"you're too energetic, too bossy, too sensitive," etc—insufficiency can become central in their conceptions of who they are.

Unfortunately, because we are so impressionable at these young ages, we can wire these negative self-beliefs and ways of talking to ourselves pretty deeply into our nervous systems. Then as we go through life, we can (and often do, because they're already in there) build on them. We can also pick up new ones. They can tangle together and gain steam. They can become very powerful.

By adulthood, however such beliefs have formed, they can feel ineluctably, obviously true.

But intellectual vulnerability invites our curiosity: are they?

Or were they important survival mechanisms that we can now release for the sake of holding beliefs that seem more true and help us live more fully?

Some Potential Costs of Negative Self-Beliefs and Talk

Do you beat yourself up? Call yourself names? Shame yourself for not meeting your own expectations? Tell yourself that other people deserve good things, but you don't?

Negative self-beliefs, begetting harsh inner dialogue, affect quality of life in tangible ways. Harsh inner dialogue can:

- Make it harder to take risks or try new things
- Undermine confidence in relationships and work
- Keep you stuck in patterns of thought, feeling, or behavior that aren't serving you
- Drain energy that could go toward growth and connection
- Make it difficult to accept compliments or acknowledge your own accomplishments

The voice in your head doesn't have to be your enemy. You can develop a more curious, compassionate relationship with yourself—one that acknowledges mistakes and limitations without harsh judgment, that honors and releases negative impulses, and that recognizes capacity for growth alongside current struggles. If you shift your understanding from "I don't deserve good things" or "I'm no good" to something more neutral or positive, you may find yourself able to relax habits of treating yourself harshly.

Curiosity as an Alternative and Antidote to Self-Criticism

With gentle curiosity, you can examine your negative self-beliefs and wonder if there are other, more accurate ways of viewing yourself.

Did you learn negative beliefs and patterns of shaming yourself for an important reason at one time? Perhaps being self-critical once helped you navigate a difficult situation or relationship. But is that strategy still serving you now?

Are your negative self-beliefs necessarily true? It seems to me that "I always mess things up," "I'm a screw up," "I'm no good," "I don't deserve good things" are not accurate. They can be helpful or feel true, but they don't seem true to me. How do they seem to you?

What alternatives might you try on for size? "I'm acceptable as I am," "I learned this thought or behavior as an appropriate response to a dangerous world," "I'm a natural being doing its best to survive and thrive, like anyone else," seem like good options to me.

Practical Exercise: Examining Your Inner Dialogue

The key here is gentle curiosity, not harsh interrogation of yourself. You're not trying to prove you're wrong about everything—you're simply exploring whether your self-beliefs are accurate and helpful, and if you'd like to try other beliefs on for size.

Name the Belief. Take a quiet moment and write down one belief you hold about yourself. It might sound like: "I'm too sensitive," "I'm not good at conflict," "I always mess things up," "I'm no good," "I don't deserve good things," or "I need to keep everyone happy." Don't filter—just notice what arises.

Trace the Origin. Ask yourself: Where might I have learned this? Was it from parents, teachers, peers, a significant experience, or messages from culture? When did I first start believing this about myself? How might it have helped me survive?

Question Its Accuracy. With intellectual vulnerability, gently ask: Is this belief accurate—or learned for survival? What evidence challenges it? When has the opposite been true? For example, "I'm too sensitive" might also mean "I'm deeply empathetic" or "I notice what others miss."

Reframe as a Question. Rewrite the belief as a question instead of a verdict. For instance:
- Instead of "I'm bad at conflict," ask: "Where did that idea come from?" and "What if I could learn new ways of navigating conflict?"
- Instead of "I'm not capable," ask: "Where did that idea come from?" and "What am I capable of that I haven't yet discovered?"

Practice Gentler Self-Talk. Speak to yourself how you would talk to someone you care about. Use warmth, curiosity, and compassion. For example: "You are allowed to be sensitive. You have capabilities you're still discovering. You are acceptable as you are."

Daily Curiosity Check. Each day for a week, pause once and ask: "What self-belief is guiding me right now? And what else might be possible?"

For More on Self-Beliefs and Life

My thoughts on self-beliefs are largely derived from the work of the brilliant psychotherapist Koorosh Rassekh. I recommend his work for exploring the nature of self-beliefs and using curiosity to live more fully and freely as yourself.

Spiritual and Existential Growth

Finally, intellectual vulnerability can transform how you approach life's biggest questions:

What gives life meaning? How should I live? What happens after death? Is there something greater than myself?

It matters. Spiritual beliefs (or existential beliefs if you don't like that language) are deeply important to us. They are how we make sense of everything. They play a key role in how we feel about what's happening in our lives every single day.

Unfortunately, because these beliefs are so important, most people resist revising them.

However: the importance of these beliefs makes them even more important to revise. There's simply more at stake. There's more to be gained by making improvements. The benefit you and others could gain from revising your beliefs could be extraordinary. You could gain more insight, peace, connection with others, maybe ultimate salvation (!). This usually far outweighs what could be lost, even while the potential loss could seem scary at first.

The Challenge of Modern Certainty about The Beyond

There are countless spiritual options today. Some experts estimate there are 20,000 variants of Christianity alone.

Most of the time, awareness of how many spiritual options there are is a source of stress. We tend to subconsciously think, or fear, that the existence of other people's beliefs invalidates or threatens our own. The philosopher Charles Taylor offers the wonderful word "fragile" to describe spiritual beliefs in the modern world. The abundance of spiritual options *fragilizes* whichever you decide to personally hold.

However: if you accept that your personal truth claims (as well as everybody else's) are on the way, you can believe what you believe while at the same time learning from the beliefs of others. Everybody's got a valid perspective to contribute. You may be more right than others, but you may not, and regardless, you can learn and grow from engaging them. Other people's beliefs can broaden and deepen your own beliefs, leading to greater understanding, growth, and hopefully meaning and peace.

Even if your beliefs are mostly correct, there's always room for growth. What are you missing about God, good, evil, sacred texts, religious experiences, philosophical arguments, and spiritual practices? There's so much other people have thought and experienced that you haven't. This includes both people in your own faith and people in other ones.

Trade Fear of Doubt for the Benefits of Exploration

Many people fear questioning their beliefs. They worry about losing community, inviting judgment from God, or feeling adrift. This is totally understandable. But it seems to me the bigger risk is stagnation. What might you miss if you never explore? What growth, love, or insight could pass you by?

If you believe in God and fear judgment for exploring, pause and consider: what if God values curiosity, questions, and exploration? What if growth and understanding are signs of engagement with the divine, not rebellion? What if there are different perspectives on God you haven't yet encountered that could enrich your relationship with God?

If you don't believe in God or other metaphysically transcendent phenomena, pause and consider: why not? Why do you believe what you believe? It's not that you're purely rational (none of us are) and have pulled the wool off your eyes, as I once assumed. There are many ways of practicing meaningfulness, spirituality, faith, and religion that are deeply rational. Exploration, reflection, and openness are not threats to truth; they are tools for deepening it, no matter what that ultimately looks like for you.

My gambit is this: even if asking questions or exploring what's out there feels uncomfortable at first, you will land somewhere better than where you started. It's true that it's a scary world out there. It's true that much is at stake. It's true that there can be real loss and pain from changing beliefs, including losing family or community.

But in my experience and observation, most people who lean into their questions and persist in seeking new answers and practices eventually land in more peace and understanding, even when the journey there is difficult.

One hard truth of existential peace is that when we neglect questions, they don't cease to exist. Burying them doesn't usually help. If, however, we honor them and give ourselves grace as we explore them, we create the possibility for deeper understanding and peace—even if the answers aren't what we expected.

Practical Exercise: Intellectual Vulnerability in Spiritual Life

1. **Identify** one spiritual or existential belief you hold tightly.
2. **Spend a week exploring** literature, perspectives, or practices that challenge or broaden it.

3. **Reflect on your reactions:** Fear, curiosity, resistance, or insight.
4. **Ask yourself:** What might I be missing? How could this help me grow?
5. **Remember:** Wondering won't estrange you from God or the truth. Giving up might.
6. **Repeat regularly.** Your beliefs are always "on the way," and your capacity for understanding deepens over time.

By approaching spiritual life with intellectual vulnerability, you can hold beliefs with integrity while remaining open to wisdom from others.

Practical Framework: The Three Domains Check-In

To integrate intellectual vulnerability across these areas, try this weekly reflection:

Physical Health: What assumption about my body or wellbeing am I ready to examine? What small, safe experiment might I try?

Self-Beliefs: What stories about myself am I telling that might be outdated or limiting? How might I approach them with curiosity rather than judgment?

Meaning and Spirit: What big questions about life am I avoiding? What perspective different from my own might enrich my understanding?

The goal isn't to overthrow everything you believe but to approach your beliefs as living, evolving touchstones you can use to help you grow into fuller ones.

The Ripple Effects

When you apply intellectual vulnerability across these domains, the effects compound. Curiosity about your health can build confidence in your ability to solve problems and help empower you with renewed energy and health. Examining limiting self-beliefs can create space for peace and growth. Openness in spiritual matters enhances your capacity for empathy and connection.

Most importantly, you develop a fundamental trust in your ability to navigate uncertainty—one of the most valuable skills in a rapidly changing world.

Recap & Reflection

Intellectual vulnerability isn't just about having better political conversations or resolving social conflicts, though it certainly helps with those challenges. It's a comprehensive approach to living that recognizes uncertainty as an opportunity rather than a threat.

When you approach your body, your self-concept, and your deepest beliefs with curiosity rather than rigid certainty, you open yourself to possibilities you might never have imagined. You transform from someone who has life figured out into someone who is actively figuring it out—and that makes all the difference.

Curiosity about big personal and existential issues not always easy. It can be painful. Sometimes it is genuinely best to forestall these kinds of explorations. But more often than not, curiosity is a great unlocker and engine of growth.

CONCLUSION
Why Not Try?

Throughout this book, we've explored how attachment to certainty—while understandable—often undermines the very things we're trying to protect: our relationships, our growth, and our ability to navigate an uncertain world with wisdom and grace.

The alternative isn't to abandon values or to become indifferent to important issues. It's to hold our beliefs with **intellectual vulnerability**: the willingness to remain curious about what we don't know, to engage with those who see the world differently, and to treat our current understanding as provisional rather than final.

It's living by *I don't know; help me grow.*

If you feel any resistance to this and hesitate to step ahead, my question for you is: why not try?

Do you want to give this a chance and see what happens?

You can start small. What if you admit you don't know much about an important issue to a friend, or have one conversation where you ask more questions than you make statements, or explore alternative views in private? Small experiments often yield surprising results. Sometimes all we need to make changes is a little bit of data from experience that shows us what's possible.

The Ongoing Challenge and Joy

The ideas in this book have grown from my own reckoning with certainty addiction. I've experienced firsthand how clinging to being right can damage relationships and limit growth. I also experienced how much richer life became when I began approaching it with genuine curiosity about what I might be missing. I'm excited to be sharing and hopefully spreading that richness with you.

Yet as much as I wish the invitation to step into an intellectually vulnerable life were an easy one, it often isn't. And it's certainly not a one-time effort. Even after practicing intellectual vulnerability for years, I still encounter topics that trigger my defensiveness, conversations that test my patience, and moments when certainty feels much more comfortable than curiosity.

But this imperfection doesn't bother me. In fact, I celebrate it. We're all on the way, and it's good to be our honest, vulnerable selves with one another. I've learned to see such moments not as failures but as opportunities to connect, learn, maybe laugh, and imagine possibilities for something better.

This is part of being human. I've come to love the journey, even with its stumbles. I love hearing about what others see from their mountaintops, then trekking over there to try to see for myself. Sometimes my walk over there is elegant. Sometimes it's awkward. One hundred percent of the time it is worth it, and beautiful.

I invite you to come alongside and delight in the adventure with me.

The Choice Ahead

Certainty promises safety but often delivers isolation. It offers the comfort of never being wrong at the cost of never growing. It provides the satisfaction of having enemies to defeat but denies the joy of discovering unexpected allies.

Intellectual vulnerability offers something different: the possibility of being surprised by what you learn, the chance to build bridges across difference, and the freedom that comes from not having to defend every detail of your worldview.

In many ways, we're all always standing in the doorway of our own cages of certainty. We can stride back into the cage and lock the door behind us, or we can step outside and look up at the big, open sky. We can glance alongside at others doing the same, and wonder: what else is out there waiting for me—for *us*—to understand?

The choice is always available to you. In every conversation, every disagreement, every moment when you encounter an idea that challenges your assumptions, you can choose curiosity or certainty, exploration or defense, growth or stagnation.

Neither choice is easy, but one leads toward isolation and rigidity while the other leads toward connection and discovery.

What will serve you best as an individual?

And what does our fractured society need from us right now?

My personal aspiration is to be just one of eight lovely billion, contributing my part with passion, humility, and love.

What do you want *your* part to be?

Some Further Reading

A Pluralistic Universe by William James

Experience and Education by John Dewey

Masters of Uncertainty: The Navy SEAL Way to Turn Stress into Success for You and Your Team by Rich Diviney

The Righteous Mind: Why Good People are Divided by Politics and Religion by Jonathan Haidt

The Art and Science of Connection: Why Social Health is the Missing Key to Living Longer, Healthier, and Happier by Kasley Killam

The Island of Knowledge: The Limits of Science and The Search for Meaning by Marcelo Gleiser

A Secular Age by Charles Taylor

Learning to Disagree: The Surprising Path to Navigating Differences with Empathy and Respect by John Inazu

I Never Thought of It That Way: How to Have Fearlessly Curious Conversations in Dangerously Divided Times by Mónica Guzmán

Exclusion and Embrace: A Theological Exploration of Identity, Otherness, and Reconciliation by Miroslav Volf

The Wisdom to Doubt: A Justification of Religious Skepticism by John Schellenberg

Acknowledgments

This book, like all my books, is thanks first and foremost to **Dorothy Ruper,** who is not only a hero to all with the privilege to know her but also a hero of curiosity for the sake of an evermore beautiful life.

I owe profound thanks to **Koorosh Rassekh** for opening my eyes to the role of self-beliefs in mental wellness as well as showing me the power of an invitational writing style.

I gratefully credit **Rich Diviney** with helping me understand more about the social function of identity and many other things about uncertainty and life besides.

I owe deep intellectual gratitude to two scholars: **Donovan Schaefer**, for helping me explore the role of emotions in belief formation and supporting me in so many other ways, and also **Stephane Madelrieux**, for his bold exploration across philosophical divides and helping me explore William James,

John Dewey, Jean Wahl, and more, playing a key role in the development of my metaphysics of time and truth (more on which in future books).

I thank the thoughtful and curious **Blake Bottrill** for offering crucial feedback on this manuscript.

Finally and not lastly, thanks go to three amazingly curious, powerful, and beautiful beings who are deeply cherished interlocutors: **Robert Seyler, Kasley Killam,** and **Aaron Lerner.** I bow with great awe to Robert's relentless and open-hearted courage on his path of healing and hope. I aspire to the heights of tenacity, kindness, grit, compassion, and grace Kasley models in her career and life. And Aaron Lerner, who once lit something inside me when he said, "I want to be good more than I want to be right," is my living proof that our greatest power lies not in our domination but our quiet wonder, patience, hope, and love.

www.ingramcontent.com/pod-product-compliance
Lightning Source LLC
Chambersburg PA
CBHW020542030426
42337CB00013B/949